# FOREWORD

The collection of "Everything Will Be Okay" travel phrasebooks published by T&P Books is designed for people traveling abroad for tourism and business. The phrasebooks contain what matters most - the essentials for basic communication. This is an indispensable set of phrases to "survive" while abroad.

This phrasebook will help you in most cases where you need to ask something, get directions, find out how much something costs, etc. It can also resolve difficult communication situations where gestures just won't help.

This book contains a lot of phrases that have been grouped according to the most relevant topics. The edition also includes a small vocabulary that contains roughly 3,000 of the most frequently used words. Another section of the phrasebook provides a gastronomical dictionary that may help you order food at a restaurant or buy groceries at the store.

Take "Everything Will Be Okay" phrasebook with you on the road and you'll have an irreplaceable traveling companion who will help you find your way out of any situation and teach you to not fear speaking with foreigners.

# TABLE OF CONTENTS

T&P Books Publishing

Travel phrasebooks collection
«Everything Will Be Okay!»

T&P Books Publishing

# PHRASEBOOK

## — DUTCH —

By Andrey Taranov

## THE MOST IMPORTANT PHRASES

This phrasebook contains
the most important
phrases and questions
for basic communication
Everything you need
to survive overseas

T&P BOOKS

**Phrasebook + 3000-word dictionary**

# English-Dutch phrasebook & topical vocabulary

By Andrey Taranov

The collection of "Everything Will Be Okay" travel phrasebooks published by T&P Books is designed for people traveling abroad for tourism and business. The phrasebooks contain what matters most - the essentials for basic communication. This is an indispensable set of phrases to "survive" while abroad.

This book also includes a small topical vocabulary that contains roughly 3,000 of the most frequently used words. Another section of the phrasebook provides a gastronomical dictionary that may help you order food at a restaurant or buy groceries at the store.

T&P Books Publishing
www.tpbooks.com

ISBN: 978-1-78492-460-7

This book is also available in E-book formats.
Please visit www.tpbooks.com or the major online bookstores.

# PRONUNCIATION

| T&P phonetic alphabet | Dutch example | English example |
| --- | --- | --- |
| [a] | plasje | shorter than in ask |
| [â] | kraag | calf, palm |
| [o], [ɔ] | zondag | drop, baught |
| [o] | geografie | pod, John |
| [ō] | oorlog | fall, bomb |
| [e] | nemen | elm, medal |
| [ē] | wreed | longer than in bell |
| [ɛ] | ketterij | man, bad |
| [ɛ:] | crème | longer than bed, fell |
| [ə] | tachtig | driver, teacher |
| [i] | alpinist | shorter than in feet |
| [ī] | referee | feet, meter |
| [ʏ] | stadhuis | fuel, tuna |
| [œ] | druif | German Hölle |
| [ø] | treurig | eternal, church |
| [u] | schroef | book |
| [ʉ] | zuchten | youth, usually |
| [ü] | minuut | fuel, tuna |
| [b] | oktober | baby, book |
| [d] | diepte | day, doctor |
| [f] | fierheid | face, food |
| [g] | golfclub | game, gold |
| [h] | horizon | home, have |
| [j] | jaar | yes, New York |
| [k] | klooster | clock, kiss |
| [l] | politiek | lace, people |
| [m] | melodie | magic, milk |
| [n] | netwerk | sang, thing |
| [p] | peper | pencil, private |
| [r] | rechter | rice, radio |
| [s] | smaak | city, boss |
| [t] | telefoon | tourist, trip |
| [v] | vijftien | very, river |
| [w] | waaier | vase, winter |

| T&P phonetic alphabet | Dutch example | English example |
|---|---|---|
| [z] | zacht | zebra, please |
| [dʒ] | manager | joke, general |
| [ʃ] | architect | machine, shark |
| [ŋ] | behang | English, ring |
| [tʃ] | beertje | church, French |
| [ʒ] | bougie | forge, pleasure |
| [x] | acht, gaan | as in Scots 'loch' |

# LIST OF ABBREVIATIONS

## English abbreviations

| | | |
|---|---|---|
| **ab.** | - | about |
| **adj** | - | adjective |
| **adv** | - | adverb |
| **anim.** | - | animate |
| **as adj** | - | attributive noun used as adjective |
| **e.g.** | - | for example |
| **etc.** | - | et cetera |
| **fam.** | - | familiar |
| **fem.** | - | feminine |
| **form.** | - | formal |
| **inanim.** | - | inanimate |
| **masc.** | - | masculine |
| **math** | - | mathematics |
| **mil.** | - | military |
| **n** | - | noun |
| **pl** | - | plural |
| **pron.** | - | pronoun |
| **sb** | - | somebody |
| **sing.** | - | singular |
| **sth** | - | something |
| **v aux** | - | auxiliary verb |
| **vi** | - | intransitive verb |
| **vi, vt** | - | intransitive, transitive verb |
| **vt** | - | transitive verb |

## Dutch abbreviations

| | | |
|---|---|---|
| **mv.** | - | plural |

## Dutch articles

| | | |
|---|---|---|
| **de** | - | common gender |
| **de/het** | - | neuter, common gender |
| **het** | - | neuter |

# T&P BOOKS

# DUTCH
# PHRASEBOOK

This section contains
important phrases that may
come in handy in various
real-life situations.
The phrasebook will help
you ask for directions, clarify
a price, buy tickets, and
order food at a restaurant

T&P Books Publishing

# PHRASEBOOK CONTENTS

T&P Books Publishing

## The bare minimum

Excuse me, ... | **Pardon, ...**
[par'dɔn, ...]

Hello. | **Hallo.**
[halɔ]

Thank you. | **Bedankt.**
[bə'dankt]

Good bye. | **Tot ziens.**
[tɔt zins]

Yes. | **Ja.**
[ja]

No. | **Nee.**
[nē]

I don't know. | **Ik weet het niet.**
[ik wēt ət nit]

Where? | Where to? | When? | **Waar? | Waarheen? | Wanneer?**
[wār? | wār'hēn? | wa'nēr?]

I need ... | **Ik heb ... nodig**
[ik hɛp ... 'nɔdəx]

I want ... | **Ik wil ...**
[ik wil ...]

Do you have ...? | **Hebt u ...?**
[hɛpt ju ...?]

Is there a ... here? | **Is hier een ...?**
[is hir en ...?]

May I ...? | **Mag ik ...?**
[max ik ...?]

..., please (polite request) | **... alstublieft**
[... alstʉ'blift]

I'm looking for ... | **Ik zoek ...**
[ik zuk ...]

restroom | **toilet**
[twa'lɛt]

ATM | **geldautomaat**
[xɛlt·autɔ'māt]

pharmacy (drugstore) | **apotheek**
[apɔ'tēk]

hospital | **ziekenhuis**
[zikənhœys]

police station | **politiebureau**
[pɔ\'litsi bʉ\'rɔ]

subway | **metro**
['metrɔ]

| | |
|---|---|
| taxi | **taxi**<br>[taksi] |
| train station | **station**<br>[sta'tsjɔn] |

| | |
|---|---|
| My name is … | **Ik heet …**<br>[ik hēt …] |
| What's your name? | **Hoe heet u?**<br>[hu hēt ju?] |
| Could you please help me? | **Kunt u me helpen alstublieft?**<br>[kunt ju mə 'hɛlpən alstu'blift?] |
| I've got a problem. | **Ik heb een probleem.**<br>[ik hɛp en prɔ'blēm] |
| I don't feel well. | **Ik voel me niet goed.**<br>[ik vul mə nit xut] |
| Call an ambulance! | **Bel een ambulance!**<br>[bɛl en ambu'lansə!] |
| May I make a call? | **Mag ik opbellen?**<br>[max ik ɔ'bɛlən?] |

| | |
|---|---|
| I'm sorry. | **Sorry.**<br>['sɔri] |
| You're welcome. | **Graag gedaan.**<br>[xrãx xə'dãn] |

| | |
|---|---|
| I, me | **Ik, mij**<br>[ik, mɛj] |
| you (inform.) | **jij**<br>[jɛj] |
| he | **hij**<br>[hɛj] |
| she | **zij**<br>[zɛj] |
| they (masc.) | **zij**<br>[zɛj] |
| they (fem.) | **zij**<br>[zɛj] |
| we | **wij**<br>[wɛj] |
| you (pl) | **jullie**<br>['juli] |
| you (sg, form.) | **u**<br>[ju] |

| | |
|---|---|
| ENTRANCE | **INGANG**<br>[inxaŋ] |
| EXIT | **UITGANG**<br>[œytxaŋ] |
| OUT OF ORDER | **BUITEN GEBRUIK**<br>[bœytən xə'brœyk] |
| CLOSED | **GESLOTEN**<br>[xə'slotən] |

| | |
|---|---|
| OPEN | **OPEN**<br>['ɔpən] |
| FOR WOMEN | **DAMES**<br>[daməs] |
| FOR MEN | **HEREN**<br>['herən] |

# Questions

| | |
|---|---|
| Where? | **Waar?**<br>[wār?] |
| Where to? | **Waarheen?**<br>[wār'hēn?] |
| Where from? | **Vanwaar?**<br>[van'wār?] |
| Why? | **Waar?**<br>[wār?] |
| For what reason? | **Waarom?**<br>[wā'rɔm?] |
| When? | **Wanneer?**<br>[wa'nēr?] |
| How long? | **Hoe lang?**<br>[hu laŋ?] |
| At what time? | **Hoe laat?**<br>[hu lāt?] |
| How much? | **Hoeveel?**<br>[huvēl?] |
| Do you have …? | **Hebt u …?**<br>[hɛpt ju …?] |
| Where is …? | **Waar is …?**<br>[wār is …?] |
| What time is it? | **Hoe laat is het?**<br>[hu lāt is ət?] |
| May I make a call? | **Mag ik opbellen?**<br>[max ik ɔ'bɛlən?] |
| Who's there? | **Wie is daar?**<br>[wi is dār?] |
| Can I smoke here? | **Mag ik hier roken?**<br>[max ik hir 'rɔkən?] |
| May I …? | **Mag ik …?**<br>[max ik …?] |

# Needs

| | |
|---|---|
| I'd like ... | **Ik zou graag ...**<br>[ik 'zau xrāx ...] |
| I don't want ... | **Ik wil niet ...**<br>[ik wil nit ...] |
| I'm thirsty. | **Ik heb dorst.**<br>[ik hɛp dɔrst] |
| I want to sleep. | **Ik wil gaan slapen.**<br>[ik wil xān 'slapən] |
| I want ... | **Ik wil ...**<br>[ik wil ...] |
| to wash up | **wassen**<br>[wasən] |
| to brush my teeth | **mijn tanden poetsen**<br>[mɛjn 'tandən 'putsən] |
| to rest a while | **even rusten**<br>[evən 'rʉstən] |
| to change my clothes | **me omkleden**<br>[mə 'ɔmkledən] |
| to go back to the hotel | **teruggaan naar het hotel**<br>[te'rʉxxān nār hɛt hɔ'tɛl] |
| to buy ... | **... kopen**<br>[... 'kɔpən] |
| to go to ... | **gaan naar ...**<br>[xān nār ...] |
| to visit ... | **bezoeken ...**<br>[bə'zukən ...] |
| to meet with ... | **ontmoeten ...**<br>[ɔnt'mutən ...] |
| to make a call | **opbellen**<br>[ɔ'bɛlən] |
| I'm tired. | **Ik ben moe.**<br>[ik bɛn mu] |
| We are tired. | **We zijn moe.**<br>[we zɛjn mu] |
| I'm cold. | **Ik heb het koud.**<br>[ik hɛp ət 'kaut] |
| I'm hot. | **Ik heb het warm.**<br>[ik hɛp ət warm] |
| I'm OK. | **Ik ben okay.**<br>[ik bɛn ɔ'kɛj] |

I need to make a call.                  **Ik moet opbellen.**
                                         [ik mut ɔ'bɛlən]

I need to go to the restroom.           **Ik moet naar het toilet.**
                                         [ik mut nãr ət twa'lɛt]

I have to go.                           **Ik moet weg.**
                                         [ik mut wɛx]

I have to go now.                       **Ik moet nu weg.**
                                         [ik mut nʉ wɛx]

## Asking for directions

| | |
|---|---|
| Excuse me, ... | **Pardon, ...**<br>[par'dɔn, ...] |
| Where is ...? | **Waar is ...?**<br>[wār is ...?] |
| Which way is ...? | **Welke richting is ...?**<br>['wɛlkə 'rixtiŋ is ...?] |
| Could you help me, please? | **Kunt u me helpen alstublieft?**<br>[kʉnt ju mə 'hɛlpən alstu'blift?] |

| | |
|---|---|
| I'm looking for ... | **Ik zoek ...**<br>[ik zuk ...] |
| I'm looking for the exit. | **Waar is de uitgang?**<br>[wār is də 'œytxaŋ?] |
| I'm going to ... | **Ik ga naar ...**<br>[ik xa nār ...] |
| Am I going the right way to ...? | **Is dit de weg naar ...?**<br>[is dit də wɛx nār ...?] |

| | |
|---|---|
| Is it far? | **Is het ver?**<br>[iz ət vɛr?] |
| Can I get there on foot? | **Kan ik er lopend naar toe?**<br>[kan ik ɛr 'lɔpənt nār tu?] |
| Can you show me on the map? | **Kunt u het op de plattegrond aanwijzen?**<br>[kʉnt ju ət ɔp də platə'xrɔnt 'ānwɛjzən?] |
| Show me where we are right now. | **Kunt u me aanwijzen waar we nu zijn?**<br>[kʉnt ju mə 'ānwɛjzən wār wə nʉ zɛjn] |

| | |
|---|---|
| Here | **Hier**<br>[hir] |
| There | **Daar**<br>[dār] |
| This way | **Deze kant uit**<br>[dezə kant 'œyt] |

| | |
|---|---|
| Turn right. | **Rechtsaf.**<br>[rɛxts'af] |
| Turn left. | **Linksaf.**<br>[linksaf] |
| first (second, third) turn | **eerste (tweede, derde) bocht**<br>[ērstə ('twēdə, 'dɛrdə) bɔxt] |
| to the right | **rechtsaf**<br>[rɛxts'af] |

to the left

**linksaf**
[linksaf]

Go straight ahead.

**Ga rechtuit.**
[xa 'rɛxtœʏt]

# Signs

| | |
|---|---|
| WELCOME! | **WELKOM!**<br>['wɛlkɔm!] |
| ENTRANCE | **INGANG**<br>[inxaŋ] |
| EXIT | **UITGANG**<br>[œʏtxaŋ] |

| | |
|---|---|
| PUSH | **DRUK**<br>[drʉk] |
| PULL | **TREK**<br>[trɛk] |
| OPEN | **OPEN**<br>['ɔpən] |
| CLOSED | **GESLOTEN**<br>[xə'slɔtən] |

| | |
|---|---|
| FOR WOMEN | **DAMES**<br>[daməs] |
| FOR MEN | **HEREN**<br>['herən] |
| GENTLEMEN, GENTS (m) | **HEREN (m)**<br>['herən] |
| WOMEN (f) | **DAMES (v)**<br>[daməs] |

| | |
|---|---|
| DISCOUNTS | **KORTINGEN**<br>['kɔrtiŋən] |
| SALE | **UITVERKOOP**<br>[œʏt'vɛrkōp] |
| FREE | **GRATIS**<br>[xratis] |
| NEW! | **NIEUW!**<br>[niu!] |
| ATTENTION! | **PAS OP!**<br>[pas ɔp!] |

| | |
|---|---|
| NO VACANCIES | **ALLE KAMERS BEZET**<br>[ale 'kamərs bə'zɛt] |
| RESERVED | **GERESERVEERD**<br>[xərezɛr'vērt] |
| ADMINISTRATION | **ADMINISTRATIE**<br>[administ'ratsi] |
| STAFF ONLY | **UITSLUITEND PERSONEEL**<br>[œʏtslœʏtənt pɛrsɔ'nēl] |

| | |
|---|---|
| BEWARE OF THE DOG! | **PAS OP VOOR DE HOND!** |
| | [pas ɔp vōr də hɔnt!] |
| NO SMOKING! | **VERBODEN TE ROKEN!** |
| | [vər'bɔdən tə 'rɔkən!] |
| DO NOT TOUCH! | **NIET AANRAKEN!** |
| | [nit 'ānrakən!] |
| DANGEROUS | **GEVAARLIJK** |
| | [xe'vārlək] |
| DANGER | **GEVAAR** |
| | [xe'vār] |
| HIGH VOLTAGE | **HOOGSPANNING** |
| | [hōxs'paniŋ] |
| NO SWIMMING! | **VERBODEN TE ZWEMMEN** |
| | [vər'bɔdən tə 'zwemən] |

| | |
|---|---|
| OUT OF ORDER | **BUITEN GEBRUIK** |
| | [bœytən xə'brœyk] |
| FLAMMABLE | **ONTVLAMBAAR** |
| | [ɔnt'flambār] |
| FORBIDDEN | **VERBODEN** |
| | [vər'bɔdən] |
| NO TRESPASSING! | **VERBODEN TOEGANG** |
| | [vər'bɔdən 'tuxaŋ] |
| WET PAINT | **NATTE VERF** |
| | [natə vɛrf] |

| | |
|---|---|
| CLOSED FOR RENOVATIONS | **GESLOTEN WEGENS VERBOUWING** |
| | [xə'slɔtən 'wexəns vər'bauwiŋ] |
| WORKS AHEAD | **WERK IN UITVOERING** |
| | [wɛrk in œyt'vuriŋ] |
| DETOUR | **OMWEG** |
| | ['ɔmwɛx] |

## Transportation. General phrases

| | |
|---|---|
| plane | **vliegtuig**<br>[vlixtœɣx] |
| train | **trein**<br>[trɛjn] |
| bus | **bus**<br>[bʉs] |
| ferry | **veerpont**<br>[vērpɔnt] |
| taxi | **taxi**<br>[taksi] |
| car | **auto**<br>[autɔ] |

| | |
|---|---|
| schedule | **dienstregeling**<br>[dinst·'rexəliŋ] |
| Where can I see the schedule? | **Waar is de dienstregeling?**<br>[wār is də dinst·'rexəliŋ?] |
| workdays (weekdays) | **werkdagen**<br>[wɛrk'daxən] |
| weekends | **weekends**<br>[wīkɛnts] |
| holidays | **vakanties**<br>[va'kantsis] |

| | |
|---|---|
| DEPARTURE | **VERTREK**<br>[vər'trɛk] |
| ARRIVAL | **AANKOMST**<br>[ānkɔmst] |
| DELAYED | **VERTRAAGD**<br>[vərt'rāxt] |
| CANCELLED | **GEANNULEERD**<br>[xəanʉ'lērt] |

| | |
|---|---|
| next (train, etc.) | **volgende**<br>['vɔlxəndə] |
| first | **eerste**<br>[ērstə] |
| last | **laatste**<br>[lātstə] |

| | |
|---|---|
| When is the next ...? | **Hoe laat gaat de volgende ...?**<br>[hu lāt xāt də 'vɔlxəndə ...?] |
| When is the first ...? | **Hoe laat gaat de eerste ...?**<br>[hu lāt xāt də 'ērstə ...?] |

When is the last ...?

**Hoe laat gaat de laatste ...?**
[hu lāt xāt də 'lātstə ...?]

transfer (change of trains, etc.)

**aansluiting**
[ānslœɣtiŋ]

to make a transfer

**overstappen**
[ɔvər'stapən]

Do I need to make a transfer?

**Moet ik overstappen?**
[mut ik ɔvər'stapən?]

## Buying tickets

Where can I buy tickets?
**Waar kan ik kaartjes kopen?**
[wār kan ik 'kārtjəs 'kɔpən?]

ticket
**kaartje**
[kārtjə]

to buy a ticket
**een kaartje kopen**
[ən 'kārtjə 'kɔpən]

ticket price
**prijs van een kaartje**
[prɛjs van en 'kārtjə]

Where to?
**Waarheen?**
[wār'hēn?]

To what station?
**Naar welk station?**
[nār wɛlk sta'tsjɔn?]

I need ...
**Ik heb ... nodig**
[ik hɛp ... 'nɔdəx]

one ticket
**een kaartje**
[ən 'kārtjə]

two tickets
**twee kaartjes**
[twē 'kārtjəs]

three tickets
**drie kaartjes**
[dri 'kārtjəs]

one-way
**enkel**
['ɛnkəl]

round-trip
**retour**
[re'tu:r]

first class
**eerste klas**
[ērstə klas]

second class
**tweede klas**
[twēdə klas]

today
**vandaag**
[van'dāx]

tomorrow
**morgen**
['mɔrxən]

the day after tomorrow
**overmorgen**
[ɔvər'mɔrxən]

in the morning
**s morgens**
[s 'mɔrxəns]

in the afternoon
**s middags**
[s 'midaxs]

in the evening
**s avonds**
[s 'avɔnts]

aisle seat

**zitplaats aan het gangpad**
[zitplãts ãn ət 'xaŋpat]

window seat

**zitplaats bij het raam**
[zitplãts bɛj ət rãm]

How much?

**Hoeveel?**
[huvēl?]

Can I pay by credit card?

**Kan ik met een creditcard betalen?**
[kan ik mɛt en 'kredit·kart bə'talən?]

# Bus

| | |
|---|---|
| bus | **bus**<br>[bʉs] |
| intercity bus | **intercity bus**<br>[inter'siti bʉs] |
| bus stop | **bushalte**<br>[bʉs'haltə] |
| Where's the nearest bus stop? | **Waar is de meest nabij gelegen bushalte?**<br>[wār is də mēst na'bɛj xə'lexən bʉs'haltə?] |

| | |
|---|---|
| number (bus ~, etc.) | **nummer**<br>[nʉmər] |
| Which bus do I take to get to ...? | **Met welke bus kan ik naar ... gaan?**<br>[mɛt 'wɛlkə bʉs kan ik nār ... xān?] |
| Does this bus go to ...? | **Gaat deze bus naar ...?**<br>[xāt 'dezə bʉs nār ...?] |
| How frequent are the buses? | **Hoe dikwijls rijden de bussen?**<br>[hu 'dikwəls 'rɛjdən də 'bʉsən?] |

| | |
|---|---|
| every 15 minutes | **om het kwartier**<br>[ɔm ət kwar'tir] |
| every half hour | **om het half uur**<br>[ɔm ət half ūr] |
| every hour | **om het uur**<br>[ɔm ət ūr] |

| | |
|---|---|
| several times a day | **verschillende keren per dag**<br>[vər'sxiləndə 'kerən pər dax] |
| ... times a day | **... keer per dag**<br>[... kēr pər dax] |

| | |
|---|---|
| schedule | **dienstregeling**<br>[dinst·'rexəliŋ] |
| Where can I see the schedule? | **Waar is de dienstregeling?**<br>[wār is də dinst·'rexəliŋ?] |

| | |
|---|---|
| When is the next bus? | **Hoe laat vertrekt de volgende bus?**<br>[hu lāt vər'trɛkt də 'vɔlxəndə bʉs?] |
| When is the first bus? | **Hoe laat vertrekt de eerste bus?**<br>[hu lāt vər'trɛkt də 'ērstə bʉs?] |
| When is the last bus? | **Hoe laat vertrekt de laatste bus?**<br>[hu lāt vər'trɛkt də 'lātstə bʉs?] |

| | |
|---|---|
| stop | **halte** |
| | [haltə] |
| next stop | **volgende halte** |
| | [vɔlxəndə 'haltə] |
| last stop (terminus) | **eindstation** |
| | [ɛjnt sta'tsjɔn] |
| Stop here, please. | **Hier stoppen alstublieft.** |
| | [hir 'stɔpən alstʉ'blift] |
| Excuse me, this is my stop. | **Pardon, dit is mijn halte.** |
| | [par'dɔn, dit is mɛjn 'haltə] |

# Train

| | |
|---|---|
| train | **trein**<br>[trɛjn] |
| suburban train | **pendeltrein**<br>['pendəl trɛjn] |
| long-distance train | **langeafstandstrein**<br>[laŋe·'afstants·trɛjn] |
| train station | **station**<br>[sta'tsjɔn] |
| Excuse me, where is the exit to the platform? | **Pardon, waar is de toegang tot het perron?**<br>[par'dɔn, wār is də 'tuxaŋ tɔt ət pɛ'rɔn?] |

| | |
|---|---|
| Does this train go to ...? | **Gaat deze trein naar ...?**<br>[xāt 'dezə trɛjn nār ...?] |
| next train | **volgende trein**<br>['vɔlxəndə trɛjn] |
| When is the next train? | **Hoe laat gaat de volgende trein?**<br>[hu lāt xāt də 'vɔlxəndə trɛjn?] |
| Where can I see the schedule? | **Waar is de dienstregeling?**<br>[wār is də dinst·'rexəliŋ?] |
| From which platform? | **Van welk perron?**<br>[van wɛlk pɛ'rɔn?] |
| When does the train arrive in ...? | **Wanneer komt de trein aan in ...?**<br>[wa'nēr kɔmt də trɛjn ān in ...?] |

| | |
|---|---|
| Please help me. | **Kunt u me helpen alstublieft?**<br>[kʉnt ju mə 'hɛlpən alstu'blift?] |
| I'm looking for my seat. | **Ik zoek mijn zitplaats.**<br>[ik zuk mɛjn 'zitplāts] |
| We're looking for our seats. | **Wij zoeken onze zitplaatsen.**<br>[wɛj 'zukən 'ɔnzə 'zitplātsen] |
| My seat is taken. | **Mijn zitplaats is bezet.**<br>[mɛjn 'zitplāts is bə'zɛt] |
| Our seats are taken. | **Onze zitplaatsen zijn bezet.**<br>[ɔnzə 'zitplātsən zɛjn bə'zɛt] |

| | |
|---|---|
| I'm sorry but this is my seat. | **Sorry, maar dit is mijn zitplaats.**<br>[sɔri, mār dit is mɛjn 'zitplāts] |
| Is this seat taken? | **Is deze zitplaats bezet?**<br>[is 'dezə 'zitplāts bə'zɛt?] |
| May I sit here? | **Mag ik hier zitten?**<br>[max ik hir 'zitən?] |

## On the train. Dialogue (No ticket)

Ticket, please.

**Uw kaartje alstublieft.**
[ʉw 'kārtjə alstʉ'blift]

I don't have a ticket.

**Ik heb geen kaartje.**
[ik hɛp xēn 'kārtjə]

I lost my ticket.

**Ik heb mijn kaartje verloren.**
[ik hɛp mɛjn 'kārtjə vər'lorən]

I forgot my ticket at home.

**Ik heb mijn kaartje thuis vergeten.**
[ik hɛp mɛjn 'kārtjə thœys vər'xetən]

You can buy a ticket from me.

**U kunt een kaartje van mij kopen.**
[ju kʉnt ən 'kārtjə van mɛj 'kopən]

You will also have to pay a fine.

**U moet ook een boete betalen.**
[ju mut ōk ən 'butə bə'talən]

Okay.

**Okay.**
[ɔ'kɛj]

Where are you going?

**Waar gaat u naartoe?**
[wār xāt ju nārtu?]

I'm going to …

**Ik ga naar …**
[ik xa nār …]

How much? I don't understand.

**Hoeveel kost het? Ik versta het niet.**
[huvēl kɔst ət? ik vərs'ta ət nit]

Write it down, please.

**Schrijf het neer alstublieft.**
[sxrɛjf ət nēr alstʉ'blift]

Okay. Can I pay with a credit card?

**Okay. Kan ik met een
creditcard betalen?**
[ɔ'kɛj. kan ik mɛt ən
'kredit·kart bə'talən?]

Yes, you can.

**Ja, dat kan.**
[ja, dat kan]

Here's your receipt.

**Hier is uw ontvangstbewijs.**
[hir is ʉw ɔnt'faŋst·bə'wɛjs]

Sorry about the fine.

**Sorry voor de boete.**
[sɔri vōr də 'butə]

That's okay. It was my fault.

**Maakt niet uit. Het is mijn schuld.**
[mākt nit œyt hɛt is mɛjn sxʉlt]

Enjoy your trip.

**Prettige reis.**
['prɛtixə rɛjs]

# Taxi

| | |
|---|---|
| taxi | **taxi**<br>[taksi] |
| taxi driver | **taxi chauffeur**<br>[taksi ʃoˈfør] |
| to catch a taxi | **een taxi nemen**<br>[ən ˈtaksi ˈnemən] |
| taxi stand | **taxistandplaats**<br>[taksi·ˈstantplāts] |
| Where can I get a taxi? | **Waar kan ik een taxi nemen?**<br>[wār kan ik en ˈtaksi ˈnemən?] |
| to call a taxi | **een taxi bellen**<br>[ən ˈtaksi ˈbɛlən] |
| I need a taxi. | **Ik heb een taxi nodig.**<br>[ik hɛp en ˈtaksi ˈnɔdəx] |

| | |
|---|---|
| Right now. | **Nu onmiddellijk.**<br>[nʉ ɔnˈmidələk] |
| What is your address (location)? | **Wat is uw adres?**<br>[wat is ʉw adˈrɛs?] |
| My address is ... | **Mijn adres is ...**<br>[mɛjn adˈrɛs is ...] |
| Your destination? | **Uw bestemming?**<br>[ʉw bəsˈtɛmiŋ?] |
| Excuse me, ... | **Pardon, ...**<br>[parˈdɔn, ...] |
| Are you available? | **Bent u vrij?**<br>[bɛnt ju vrɛj?] |
| How much is it to get to ...? | **Hoeveel kost het naar ...?**<br>[huvēl kɔst ət nār ...?] |
| Do you know where it is? | **Weet u waar dit is?**<br>[wēt ju wār dit is?] |

| | |
|---|---|
| Airport, please. | **Luchthaven alstublieft.**<br>[lʉxtˈhavən alstʉˈblift] |
| Stop here, please. | **Hier stoppen alstublieft.**<br>[hir ˈstɔpən alstʉˈblift] |
| It's not here. | **Het is niet hier.**<br>[hɛt is nit hir] |
| This is the wrong address. | **Dit is het verkeerde adres.**<br>[dit is ət vərˈkērdə adˈrɛs] |
| Turn left. | **Linksaf.**<br>[linksaf] |
| Turn right. | **Rechtsaf.**<br>[rɛxtsˈaf] |

How much do I owe you?

**Hoeveel ben ik u schuldig?**
[huvēl bɛn ik ju 'sxʉldəx?]

I'd like a receipt, please.

**Kan ik een bon krijgen alstublieft.**
[kan ik en bɔn 'krɛjxən alstʉ'blift]

Keep the change.

**Hou het kleingeld maar.**
[hau ət 'klɛjnxɛlt mãr]

Would you please wait for me?

**Wil u even op mij wachten?**
[wil ju 'evən ɔp mɛj 'waxtən?]

five minutes

**vijf minuten**
[vɛjf mi'nʉtən]

ten minutes

**tien minuten**
[tin mi'nʉtən]

fifteen minutes

**vijftien minuten**
[vɛjftin mi'nʉtən]

twenty minutes

**twintig minuten**
[twintəx mi'nʉtən]

half an hour

**een half uur**
[en half ūr]

# Hotel

| | |
|---|---|
| Hello. | **Hallo.**<br>[halɔ] |
| My name is … | **Ik heet …**<br>[ik hēt …] |
| I have a reservation. | **Ik heb gereserveerd.**<br>[ik hɛp xərezɛr'vērt] |
| I need … | **Ik heb … nodig**<br>[ik hɛp … 'nɔdəx] |
| a single room | **een enkele kamer**<br>[en 'ɛnkelə 'kamər] |
| a double room | **een tweepersoons kamer**<br>[en twē·pɛr'sōns 'kamər] |
| How much is that? | **Hoeveel kost dat?**<br>[huvēl kɔst dat?] |
| That's a bit expensive. | **Dat is nogal duur.**<br>[dat is 'nɔxal dūr] |
| Do you have anything else? | **Zijn er geen andere mogelijkheden?**<br>[zɛjn ɛr xēn 'anderə 'mɔxələkhedən?] |
| I'll take it. | **Die neem ik.**<br>[di nēm ik] |
| I'll pay in cash. | **Ik betaal contant.**<br>[ik bə'tāl kɔn'tant] |
| I've got a problem. | **Ik heb een probleem.**<br>[ik hɛp en prɔ'blēm] |
| My … is broken. | **Mijn … is stuk.**<br>[mɛjn … is stʉk] |
| My … is out of order. | **Mijn … doet het niet meer.**<br>[mɛjn … dut ət nit mēr] |
| TV | **TV**<br>[te've] |
| air conditioner | **airco**<br>['ɛrkɔ] |
| tap | **kraan**<br>[krān] |
| shower | **douche**<br>[duʃ] |
| sink | **lavabo**<br>[lava'bɔ] |
| safe | **brandkast**<br>[brantkast] |

| | |
|---|---|
| door lock | **deurslot**<br>['dørslɔt] |
| electrical outlet | **stopcontact**<br>[stɔp kɔn'takt] |
| hairdryer | **haardroger**<br>[hãr·drɔxər] |

| | |
|---|---|
| I don't have … | **Ik heb geen …**<br>[ik hɛp xēn …] |
| water | **water**<br>[watər] |
| light | **licht**<br>[lixt] |
| electricity | **stroom**<br>[strõm] |

| | |
|---|---|
| Can you give me …? | **Kunt u mij een … bezorgen?**<br>[kʉnt ju mɛj en … bə'zɔrxən?] |
| a towel | **een handdoek**<br>[en 'handuk] |
| a blanket | **een deken**<br>[en 'dekən] |
| slippers | **pantoffels**<br>[pan'tɔfəls] |
| a robe | **een badjas**<br>[en badjas] |
| shampoo | **shampoo**<br>[ʃʌmpõ] |
| soap | **zeep**<br>[zēp] |

| | |
|---|---|
| I'd like to change rooms. | **Ik wil van kamer veranderen.**<br>[ik wil van 'kamər və'randerən] |
| I can't find my key. | **Ik kan mijn sleutel niet vinden.**<br>[ik kan mɛjn 'sløtel nit 'vindən] |
| Could you open my room, please? | **Kunt u mijn kamer openen alstublieft?**<br>[kʉnt ju mɛjn 'kamər 'ɔpenən alstʉ'blift?] |
| Who's there? | **Wie is daar?**<br>[wi is dãr?] |
| Come in! | **Kom binnen!**<br>[kɔm 'binən!] |
| Just a minute! | **Een ogenblikje!**<br>[en 'ɔxənblikje!] |
| Not right now, please. | **Niet op dit moment alstublieft.**<br>[nit ɔp dit mɔ'mɛnt alstʉ'blift] |

| | |
|---|---|
| Come to my room, please. | **Kom naar mijn kamer alstublieft.**<br>[kɔm nãr mɛjn 'kamər alstʉ'blift] |
| I'd like to order food service. | **Kan ik room service krijgen.**<br>[kan ik rõm 'sø:rvis 'krɛjxən] |
| My room number is … | **Mijn kamernummer is …**<br>[mɛjn 'kamər·'nʉmer is …] |

I'm leaving ...

**Ik vertrek ...**
[ik vər'trɛk ...]

We're leaving ...

**Wij vertrekken ...**
[wɛj vər'trɛkən ...]

right now

**nu onmiddellijk**
[nʉ ɔn'midələk]

this afternoon

**vanmiddag**
[van'midax]

tonight

**vanavond**
[va'navɔnt]

tomorrow

**morgen**
['mɔrxən]

tomorrow morning

**morgenochtend**
['mɔrxən 'ɔxtənt]

tomorrow evening

**morgenavond**
[mɔrxən 'avɔnt]

the day after tomorrow

**overmorgen**
[ɔvər'mɔrxən]

I'd like to pay.

**Ik zou willen afrekenen.**
[ik 'zau 'wilən 'afrekənən]

Everything was wonderful.

**Alles was uitstekend.**
[aləs was œyts'tekənt]

Where can I get a taxi?

**Waar kan ik een taxi nemen?**
[wār kan ik en 'taksi 'nemən?]

Would you call a taxi for me, please?

**Wil u alstublieft een taxi bestellen?**
[wil ju alstʉ'blift en 'taksi bəs'tɛlən?]

## Restaurant

Can I look at the menu, please? **Kan ik het menu zien alstublieft?**
[kan ik ət me'nʉ zin alstʉ'blift?]

Table for one. **Een tafel voor één persoon.**
[en 'tafəl vör en pɛr'sôn]

There are two (three, four) of us. **We zijn met z'n tweeën (drieën, vieren).**
[we zɛjn mɛt zən 'twēɛn ('driɛn, 'virən)]

Smoking **Roken**
['rɔkən]

No smoking **Niet roken**
[nit 'rɔkən]

Excuse me! (addressing a waiter) **Hallo! Pardon!**
[halɔ! par'dɔn!]

menu **menu**
[me'nʉ]

wine list **wijnkaart**
[wɛjnkārt]

The menu, please. **Het menu alstublieft.**
[hɛt me'nʉ alstʉ'blift]

Are you ready to order? **Bent u zover om te bestellen?**
[bɛnt ju 'zɔvər ɔm tə bəs'tɛlən?]

What will you have? **Wat wenst u?**
[wat wɛnst ju?]

I'll have … **Voor mij …**
[vör mɛj …]

I'm a vegetarian. **Ik ben vegetariër.**
[ik bɛn vexə'tarijər]

meat **vlees**
[vlēs]

fish **vis**
[vis]

vegetables **groente**
['xruntə]

Do you have vegetarian dishes? **Hebt u vegetarische gerechten?**
[hɛpt ju vexə'tarisə xə'rɛxtən?]

I don't eat pork. **Ik eet niet varkensvlees.**
[ik ēt nit 'varkənsvlēs]

He /she/ doesn't eat meat. **Hij /zij/ eet geen vlees.**
[hɛj /zɛj/ ēt xēn vlēs]

I am allergic to ...

**Ik ben allergisch voor ...**
[ik bɛn a'lerxis vōr ...]

Would you please bring me ...

**Wil u mij ... brengen**
[wil ju mɛj ... b'rɛŋən]

salt | pepper | sugar

**zout | peper | suiker**
[zaut | 'pepər | 'sœʏkər]

coffee | tea | dessert

**koffie | thee | dessert**
[kɔfi | tē | dɛ'sɛːr]

water | sparkling | plain

**water | met prik | gewoon**
[watər | mɛt prik | xə'wōn]

a spoon | fork | knife

**een lepel | vork | mes**
[en 'lepəl | vɔrk | mɛs]

a plate | napkin

**een bord | servet**
[en bɔrt | sɛr'vɛt]

---

Enjoy your meal!

**Smakelijk!**
[smakələk!]

One more, please.

**Nog een alstublieft.**
[nɔx en alstʉ'blift]

It was very delicious.

**Het was heerlijk.**
[hɛt was 'hērlək]

---

check | change | tip

**rekening | wisselgeld | fooi**
[rekəniŋ | 'wisəl·xɛlt | fōj]

Check, please.
(Could I have the check, please?)

**De rekening alstublieft.**
[də 'rekəniŋ alstu'blift]

Can I pay by credit card?

**Kan ik met een creditcard betalen?**
[kan ik mɛt en 'kredit·kart bə'talən?]

I'm sorry, there's a mistake here.

**Sorry, hier is een fout.**
[sɔri, hir iz en 'faut]

## Shopping

Can I help you?

**Waarmee kan ik u van dienst zijn?**
[wār'mē kan ik ju van dinst zɛjn?]

Do you have ...?

**Hebt u ...?**
[hɛpt ju ...?]

I'm looking for ...

**Ik zoek ...**
[ik zuk ...]

I need ...

**Ik heb ... nodig**
[ik hɛp ... 'nɔdəx]

I'm just looking.

**Ik kijk even.**
[ik kɛjk 'evən]

We're just looking.

**Wij kijken even.**
[wɛj 'kɛjkən 'evən]

I'll come back later.

**Ik kom wat later terug.**
[ik kɔm wat 'latər te'rux]

We'll come back later.

**We komen later terug.**
[we 'kɔmən 'latər te'rux]

discounts | sale

**korting | uitverkoop**
[kɔrtiŋ | 'œʏtverkōp]

Would you please show me ...

**Kunt u mij ... laten zien alstublieft?**
[kʉnt ju mɛj ... 'latən zin alstʉ'blift?]

Would you please give me ...

**Kunt u mij ... geven alstublieft?**
[kʉnt ju mɛj ... 'xevən alstʉ'blift?]

Can I try it on?

**Kan ik dit passen?**
[kan ik dit 'pasən?]

Excuse me, where's the fitting room?

**Pardon, waar is de paskamer?**
[par'dɔn, wār is də 'pas·kamər?]

Which color would you like?

**Welke kleur wenst u?**
['wɛlkə 'klør wɛnst ju?]

size | length

**maat | lengte**
[māt | 'leŋtə]

How does it fit?

**Past het?**
[past ət?]

How much is it?

**Hoeveel kost het?**
[huvēl kɔst ət?]

That's too expensive.

**Dat is te duur.**
[dat is tə dūr]

I'll take it.

**Ik neem het.**
[ik nēm ət]

Excuse me, where do I pay?

**Pardon, waar moet ik betalen?**
[par'dɔn, wār mut ik bə'talən?]

Will you pay in cash or credit card?

**Betaalt u contant of met een creditcard?**
[be'tālt ju kɔn'tant ɔf mɛt en 'kredit·kart?]

In cash | with credit card

**contant | met een creditcard**
[kɔn'tant | mɛt en 'kredit·kart]

Do you want the receipt?

**Wil u een kwitantie?**
[wil ju en kwi'tantsi?]

Yes, please.

**Ja graag.**
[ja xrāx]

No, it's OK.

**Nee, hoeft niet.**
[nē, huft nit]

Thank you. Have a nice day!

**Bedankt. Een fijne dag verder!**
[be'dankt. en 'fɛjne dax 'vɛrdər!]

## In town

| | |
|---|---|
| Excuse me, please. | **Pardon, …**<br>[par'dɔn, …] |
| I'm looking for … | **Ik ben op zoek naar …**<br>[ik bɛn ɔp zuk nãr …] |
| the subway | **de metro**<br>[də 'metrɔ] |
| my hotel | **mijn hotel**<br>[mɛjn hɔ'tɛl] |
| the movie theater | **de bioscoop**<br>[də biɔ'skõp] |
| a taxi stand | **een taxistandplaats**<br>[en 'taksi·'stantplãts] |
| an ATM | **een geldautomaat**<br>[en xɛlt·autɔ'mãt] |
| a foreign exchange office | **een wisselagent**<br>[en 'wisəl·a'xɛnt] |
| an internet café | **een internet café**<br>[en 'intərnɛt ka'fe] |
| … street | **… straat**<br>[… strãt] |
| this place | **dit adres**<br>[dit ad'rɛs] |
| Do you know where … is? | **Weet u waar … is?**<br>[wẽt ju wãr … is?] |
| Which street is this? | **Welke straat is dit?**<br>[wɛlkə strãt is dit?] |
| Show me where we are right now. | **Kunt u me aanwijzen waar we nu zijn?**<br>[kʉnt ju mə 'ãnwɛjzən wãr wə nʉ zɛjn] |
| Can I get there on foot? | **Kan ik er lopend naar toe?**<br>[kan ik ɛr 'lɔpənt nãr tu?] |
| Do you have a map of the city? | **Hebt u een plattegrond van de stad?**<br>[hɛpt ju en platə'xrɔnt van də stat?] |
| How much is a ticket to get in? | **Hoeveel kost de toegang?**<br>[huvẽl kɔst də 'tuxaŋ?] |
| Can I take pictures here? | **Kan ik hier foto's maken?**<br>[kan ik hir 'fotɔs 'makən?] |
| Are you open? | **Bent u open?**<br>[bɛnt ju 'ɔpən?] |

When do you open?

**Hoe laat gaat u open?**
[hu lāt xāt ju 'ɔpən?]

When do you close?

**Hoe laat sluit u?**
[hu lāt slœʏt ju?]

# Money

| | |
|---|---|
| money | **geld**<br>[xɛlt] |
| cash | **contant**<br>[kɔn'tant] |
| paper money | **bankbiljetten**<br>[bank·bi'ljetən] |
| loose change | **kleingeld**<br>[klɛjn·xɛlt] |
| check \| change \| tip | **rekening \| wisselgeld \| fooi**<br>[rekənɪŋ \| 'wisəl·xɛlt \| fōj] |
| credit card | **creditcard**<br>[kredit·kart] |
| wallet | **portemonnee**<br>[pɔrtəmɔ'nē] |
| to buy | **kopen**<br>['kɔpən] |
| to pay | **betalen**<br>[bə'talən] |
| fine | **boete**<br>['butə] |
| free | **gratis**<br>[xratis] |
| Where can I buy …? | **Waar kan ik … kopen?**<br>[wār kan ik … 'kɔpən?] |
| Is the bank open now? | **Is de bank nu open?**<br>[is də bank nʉ 'ɔpən?] |
| When does it open? | **Hoe laat gaat hij open?**<br>[hu lāt xāt hɛj 'ɔpən?] |
| When does it close? | **Hoe laat sluit hij?**<br>[hu lāt slœyt hɛj?] |
| How much? | **Hoeveel?**<br>[huvēl?] |
| How much is this? | **Hoeveel kost dit?**<br>[huvēl kɔst dit?] |
| That's too expensive. | **Dat is te duur.**<br>[dat is tə dūr] |
| Excuse me, where do I pay? | **Pardon, waar moet ik betalen?**<br>[par'dɔn, wār mut ik bə'talən?] |
| Check, please. | **De rekening alstublieft.**<br>[də 'rekənɪŋ alstʉ'blift] |

Can I pay by credit card? **Kan ik met een creditcard betalen?**
[kan ik mɛt en 'kredit·kart bə'talən?]

Is there an ATM here? **Is hier een geldautomaat?**
[is hir en xɛlt·autɔ'māt?]

I'm looking for an ATM. **Ik zoek een geldautomaat.**
[ik zuk en xɛlt·autɔ'māt]

---

I'm looking for a foreign exchange office. **Ik zoek een wisselagent.**
[ik zuk en 'wisəl a'xɛnt]

I'd like to change ... **Ik zou ... willen wisselen.**
[ik 'zau ... 'wilən 'wisələn]

What is the exchange rate? **Wat is de wisselkoers?**
[wat is də 'wisəl·kurs?]

Do you need my passport? **Hebt u mijn paspoort nodig?**
[hɛpt ju mɛjn 'paspōrt 'nɔdəx?]

# Time

| | |
|---|---|
| What time is it? | **Hoe laat is het?**<br>[hu lāt is ət?] |
| When? | **Wanneer?**<br>[wa'nēr?] |
| At what time? | **Hoe laat?**<br>[hu lāt?] |
| now \| later \| after ... | **nu \| later \| na ...**<br>[nʉ \| 'latər \| na ...] |
| one o'clock | **een uur**<br>[en ūr] |
| one fifteen | **kwart over een**<br>[kwart 'ɔvər en] |
| one thirty | **half twee**<br>[half twē] |
| one forty-five | **kwart voor twee**<br>[kwart vōr twē] |
| one \| two \| three | **een \| twee \| drie**<br>[en \| twē \| dri] |
| four \| five \| six | **vier \| vijf \| zes**<br>[vir \| vɛjf \| zɛs] |
| seven \| eight \| nine | **zeven \| acht \| negen**<br>[zevən \| axt \| 'nexən] |
| ten \| eleven \| twelve | **tien \| elf \| twaalf**<br>[tin \| ɛlf \| twālf] |
| in ... | **binnen ...**<br>['binən ...] |
| five minutes | **vijf minuten**<br>[vɛjf mi'nʉtən] |
| ten minutes | **tien minuten**<br>[tin mi'nʉtən] |
| fifteen minutes | **vijftien minuten**<br>[vɛjftin mi'nʉtən] |
| twenty minutes | **twintig minuten**<br>[twintəx mi'nʉtən] |
| half an hour | **een half uur**<br>[en half ūr] |
| an hour | **een uur**<br>[en ūr] |

| | |
|---|---|
| in the morning | **s ochtends**<br>[s 'ɔxtənts] |
| early in the morning | **s ochtends vroeg**<br>[s 'ɔxtənts vrux] |
| this morning | **vanmorgen**<br>[van'mɔrxən] |
| tomorrow morning | **morgenochtend**<br>['mɔrxən 'ɔxtənt] |
| in the middle of the day | **in het midden van de dag**<br>[in ət 'midən van də dax] |
| in the afternoon | **s middags**<br>[s 'midaxs] |
| in the evening | **s avonds**<br>[s 'avɔnts] |
| tonight | **vanavond**<br>[va'navɔnt] |
| at night | **s avonds**<br>[s 'avɔnts] |
| yesterday | **gisteren**<br>['xistərən] |
| today | **vandaag**<br>[van'dãx] |
| tomorrow | **morgen**<br>['mɔrxən] |
| the day after tomorrow | **overmorgen**<br>[ɔvər'mɔrxən] |
| What day is it today? | **Wat is het vandaag?**<br>[wat is ət van'dãx?] |
| It's ... | **Het is ...**<br>[hɛt is ...] |
| Monday | **maandag**<br>[mãndax] |
| Tuesday | **dinsdag**<br>[dinzdax] |
| Wednesday | **woensdag**<br>[wunzdax] |
| Thursday | **donderdag**<br>[dɔndərdax] |
| Friday | **vrijdag**<br>[vrɛjdax] |
| Saturday | **zaterdag**<br>[zatərdax] |
| Sunday | **zondag**<br>[zɔndax] |

## Greetings. Introductions

Hello.

**Hallo.**
[halɔ]

Pleased to meet you.

**Aangenaam.**
[ānxənām]

Me too.

**Insgelijks.**
['insxeləks]

I'd like you to meet ...

**Mag ik u voorstellen aan ...**
[max ik ju 'vōrstɛlən ān ...]

Nice to meet you.

**Aangenaam.**
[ānxənām]

How are you?

**Hoe gaat het met u?**
[hu xāt ət mɛt ju?]

My name is ...

**Ik heet ...**
[ik hēt ...]

His name is ...

**Dit is ...**
[dit is ...]

Her name is ...

**Dit is ...**
[dit is ...]

What's your name?

**Hoe heet u?**
[hu hēt ju?]

What's his name?

**Hoe heet hij?**
[hu hēt hɛj?]

What's her name?

**Hoe heet zij?**
[hu hēt zɛj?]

What's your last name?

**Wat is uw achternaam?**
[wat is ʉw 'axtər·nām?]

You can call me ...

**Noem mij maar ...**
[num mɛj mār ...]

Where are you from?

**Vanwaar komt u?**
[van'wār kɔmt ju?]

I'm from ...

**Ik kom van ...**
[ik kɔm van ...]

What do you do for a living?

**Wat is uw beroep?**
[wat is ʉw bə'rup?]

Who is this?

**Wie is dit?**
[wi is dit?]

Who is he?

**Wie is hij?**
[wi is hɛj?]

Who is she?

**Wie is zij?**
[wi is zɛj?]

Who are they?

**Wie zijn zij?**
[wi zɛjn zɛj?]

| This is ... | **Dit is ...** |
| | [dit is ...] |
| my friend (masc.) | **mijn vriend** |
| | [mɛjn vrint] |
| my friend (fem.) | **mijn vriendin** |
| | [mɛjn vrin'din] |
| my husband | **mijn man** |
| | [mɛjn man] |
| my wife | **mijn vrouw** |
| | [mɛjn 'vrau] |

| my father | **mijn vader** |
| | [mɛjn 'vadər] |
| my mother | **mijn moeder** |
| | [mɛjn 'mudər] |
| my brother | **mijn broer** |
| | [mɛjn brur] |
| my sister | **mijn zuster** |
| | [mɛjn 'zʉstər] |
| my son | **mijn zoon** |
| | [mɛjn zõn] |
| my daughter | **mijn dochter** |
| | [mɛjn 'dɔxtər] |

| This is our son. | **Dit is onze zoon.** |
| | [dit is 'ɔnzə zõn] |
| This is our daughter. | **Dit is onze dochter.** |
| | [dit is 'ɔnzə 'dɔxtər] |
| These are my children. | **Dit zijn mijn kinderen.** |
| | [dit zɛjn 'mɛjn 'kindərən] |
| These are our children. | **Dit zijn onze kinderen.** |
| | [dit zɛjn 'ɔnzə 'kindərən] |

## Farewells

| | |
|---|---|
| Good bye! | **Tot ziens!** |
| | [tɔt zins!] |
| Bye! (inform.) | **Doei!** |
| | [dui!] |
| See you tomorrow. | **Tot morgen.** |
| | [tɔt 'mɔrxən] |
| See you soon. | **Tot binnenkort.** |
| | [tɔt binə'kɔrt] |
| See you at seven. | **Tot om zeven uur.** |
| | [tɔt ɔm 'zevən ūr] |

| | |
|---|---|
| Have fun! | **Veel plezier!** |
| | [vēl plə'zīr!] |
| Talk to you later. | **Tot straks.** |
| | [tɔt straks] |
| Have a nice weekend. | **Prettig weekend.** |
| | [prɛtəx 'wīkɛnt] |
| Good night. | **Goede nacht.** |
| | [xudə naxt] |

| | |
|---|---|
| It's time for me to go. | **ik moet opstappen.** |
| | [ik mut 'ɔpstapən] |
| I have to go. | **Ik moet weg.** |
| | [ik mut wɛx] |
| I will be right back. | **ik ben zo terug.** |
| | [ik bɛn zɔ te'rʉx] |

| | |
|---|---|
| It's late. | **Het is al laat.** |
| | [hɛt is al lāt] |
| I have to get up early. | **Ik moet vroeg op.** |
| | [ik mut vrux ɔp] |
| I'm leaving tomorrow. | **Ik vertrek morgen.** |
| | [ik vər'trɛk 'mɔrxən] |
| We're leaving tomorrow. | **Wij vertrekken morgen.** |
| | [wɛj vər'trɛkən 'mɔrxən] |

| | |
|---|---|
| Have a nice trip! | **Prettige reis!** |
| | ['prɛtixə rɛjs!] |
| It was nice meeting you. | **Het was fijn u te leren kennen.** |
| | [hɛt was fɛjn ju tə 'lerən 'kɛnən] |
| It was nice talking to you. | **Het was een prettig gesprek.** |
| | [hɛt was en 'prɛtəx xe'sprɛk] |
| Thanks for everything. | **Dank u wel voor alles.** |
| | [dank ju wɛl vōr 'aləs] |

I had a very good time. | **ik heb ervan genoten.**
[ik hɛp ɛr'van xə'nɔtən]

We had a very good time. | **Wij hebben ervan genoten.**
[wɛj 'hɛbən ɛr'van xə'nɔtən]

It was really great. | **Het was bijzonder leuk.**
[hɛt was bi'zɔndər 'løk]

I'm going to miss you. | **Ik ga je missen.**
[ik xa je 'misən]

We're going to miss you. | **Wij gaan je missen.**
[wɛj xãn je 'misən]

Good luck! | **Veel succes!**
[vēl sʉk'sɛs!]

Say hi to ... | **De groeten aan ...**
[də 'xrutən ãn ...]

## Foreign language

I don't understand.

**Ik versta het niet.**
[ik vər'sta ət nit]

Write it down, please.

**Schrijf het neer alstublieft.**
[sxrɛjf ət nẽr alstu'blift]

Do you speak ...?

**Spreekt u ...?**
[sprẽkt ju ...?]

I speak a little bit of ...

**Ik spreek een beetje ...**
[ik sprẽk en 'bẽtjə ...]

English

**Engels**
['ɛŋəls]

Turkish

**Turks**
[tʉrks]

Arabic

**Arabisch**
[a'rabis]

French

**Frans**
[frans]

German

**Duits**
[dœyts]

Italian

**Italiaans**
[itali'ãns]

Spanish

**Spaans**
[spãns]

Portuguese

**Portugees**
[pɔrtʉ'xẽs]

Chinese

**Chinees**
[ʃi'nẽs]

Japanese

**Japans**
[ja'pans]

Can you repeat that, please.

**Kunt u dat herhalen alstublieft.**
[kʉnt ju dat hɛr'halən alstu'blift]

I understand.

**Ik versta het.**
[ik vər'sta ət]

I don't understand.

**Ik versta het niet.**
[ik vər'sta ət nit]

Please speak more slowly.

**Spreek wat langzamer alstublieft.**
[sprẽk wat 'laŋzamər alstu'blift]

Is that correct? (Am I saying it right?)

**Is dat juist?**
[is dat jœyst?]

What is this? (What does this mean?)

**Wat is dit?**
[wat is dit?]

## Apologies

Excuse me, please.

**Excuseer me alstublieft.**
[ɛkskʉ'zēr mə alstʉ'blift]

I'm sorry.

**Sorry.**
['sɔri]

I'm really sorry.

**Het spijt me.**
[hɛt spɛjt mə]

Sorry, it's my fault.

**Sorry, het is mijn schuld.**
[sɔri, hɛt is mɛjn sxʉlt]

My mistake.

**Mijn schuld.**
[mɛjn sxʉlt]

May I ...?

**Mag ik ...?**
[max ik ...?]

Do you mind if I ...?

**Is het goed dat ...?**
[iz ət xut dat ...?]

It's OK.

**Het is okay.**
[hɛt is ɔ'kɛj]

It's all right.

**Maakt niet uit.**
[mākt nit œʏt]

Don't worry about it.

**Maak je geen zorgen.**
[māk je xēn 'zɔrxən]

## Agreement

Yes.                        **Ja.**
                            [ja]

Yes, sure.                  **Ja zeker.**
                            [ja 'zekər]

OK (Good!)                  **Goed!**
                            [xut!]

Very well.                  **Uitstekend.**
                            [œyt'stekənt]

Certainly!                  **Zeker weten!**
                            ['zekər 'wetən!]

I agree.                    **Ik ga akkoord.**
                            [ik xa a'kõrt]

That's correct.             **Precies.**
                            [prə'sis]

That's right.               **Juist.**
                            [jœyst]

You're right.               **Je hebt gelijk.**
                            [je hɛpt xə'lɛjk]

I don't mind.               **Ik doe het graag.**
                            [ik du ət xrãx]

Absolutely right.           **Dat is juist.**
                            [dat is jœyst]

It's possible.              **Dat is mogelijk.**
                            [dat is 'mɔxələk]

That's a good idea.         **Dat is een goed idee.**
                            [dat is ɛn xut i'dē]

I can't say no.             **Ik kan niet nee zeggen.**
                            [ik kan nit nē 'zɛxən]

I'd be happy to.            **Met genoegen.**
                            [mɛt xə'nuxən]

With pleasure.              **Graag.**
                            [xrãx]

## Refusal. Expressing doubt

No.
**Nee.**
[nē]

Certainly not.
**Beslist niet.**
[bəs'list nit]

I don't agree.
**Daar ben ik het niet mee eens.**
[dār bɛn ik ət nit mē ēns]

I don't think so.
**Dat geloof ik niet.**
[dat xe'lōf ik nit]

It's not true.
**Dat is niet waar.**
[dat is nit wār]

You are wrong.
**U maakt een fout.**
[ju mākt en 'faut]

I think you are wrong.
**Ik denk dat u een fout maakt.**
[ik dɛnk dat ju en 'faut mākt]

I'm not sure.
**Ik weet het niet zeker.**
[ik wēt ət nit 'zekər]

It's impossible.
**Het is onmogelijk.**
[hɛt is ɔn'mɔxələk]

Nothing of the kind (sort)!
**Beslist niet!**
[bəs'list nit!]

The exact opposite.
**Precies het tegenovergestelde!**
[prə'sis hɛt 'texən·'ɔvərxəstɛldə!]

I'm against it.
**Ik ben er tegen.**
[ik bɛn ɛr 'texən]

I don't care.
**Ik geef er niet om.**
[ik xēf ɛr nit ɔm]

I have no idea.
**Ik heb geen idee.**
[ik hɛp xēn i'dē]

I doubt it.
**Dat betwijfel ik.**
[dat bet'wɛjfəl ik]

Sorry, I can't.
**Sorry, ik kan niet.**
[sɔri, ik kan nit]

Sorry, I don't want to.
**Sorry, ik wil niet.**
['sɔri, ik wil nit]

Thank you, but I don't need this.
**Dank u, maar ik heb dit niet nodig.**
[dank ju, mār ik hɛp dit nit 'nɔdəx]

It's getting late.
**Het wordt laat.**
[hɛt wɔrt lāt]

I have to get up early.

**Ik moet vroeg op.**
[ik mut vrux ɔp]

I don't feel well.

**Ik voel me niet lekker.**
[ik vul mə nit 'lɛkər]

# Expressing gratitude

| | |
|---|---|
| Thank you. | **Bedankt.**<br>[bə'dankt] |
| Thank you very much. | **Heel erg bedankt.**<br>[hēl ɛrx bə'dankt] |
| I really appreciate it. | **Ik stel dit zeer op prijs.**<br>[ik stel dit zēr ɔp prɛjs] |
| I'm really grateful to you. | **Ik ben u erg dankbaar.**<br>[ik bɛn ju ɛrx 'dankbār] |
| We are really grateful to you. | **Wij zijn u erg dankbaar.**<br>[wɛj zɛjn ju ɛrx 'dankbār] |
| Thank you for your time. | **Bedankt voor uw tijd.**<br>[bə'dankt vōr ʉw tɛjt] |
| Thanks for everything. | **Dank u wel voor alles.**<br>[dank ju wɛl vōr 'aləs] |
| Thank you for ... | **Bedankt voor ...**<br>[bə'dankt vōr ...] |
| your help | **uw hulp**<br>[ʉw hʉlp] |
| a nice time | **een leuke dag**<br>[en 'løkə dax] |
| a wonderful meal | **een heerlijke maaltijd**<br>[en 'hērlɛkə 'māltɛjt] |
| a pleasant evening | **een prettige avond**<br>[en 'prɛtixə 'avɔnt] |
| a wonderful day | **een prettige dag**<br>[en 'prɛtixə dax] |
| an amazing journey | **een fantastische reis**<br>[en fan'tastise rɛjs] |
| Don't mention it. | **Graag gedaan.**<br>[xrāx xə'dān] |
| You are welcome. | **Graag gedaan.**<br>[xrāx xə'dān] |
| Any time. | **Graag gedaan.**<br>[xrāx xə'dān] |
| My pleasure. | **Tot uw dienst.**<br>[tɔt ʉw dinst] |
| Forget it. | **Graag gedaan.**<br>[xrāx xə'dān] |
| Don't worry about it. | **Maak je geen zorgen.**<br>[māk je xēn 'zɔrxən] |

## Congratulations. Best wishes

Congratulations!

**Gefeliciteerd!**
[xəfelisi'tērt!]

Happy birthday!

**Gefeliciteerd met je verjaardag!**
[xəfelisi'tērt met je və'rjārdax!]

Merry Christmas!

**Prettig Kerstfeest!**
[prɛtəx 'kɛrstfēst!]

Happy New Year!

**Gelukkig Nieuwjaar!**
[xə'lukəx 'niu'jār!]

Happy Easter!

**Vrolijk Paasfeest!**
[vrɔlək 'pāsfēst!]

Happy Hanukkah!

**Gelukkig Chanoeka!**
[xə'lukəx 'xanuka!]

I'd like to propose a toast.

**Ik wil een heildronk uitbrengen.**
[ik wil en 'hɛjldrɔnk 'œytbreŋen]

Cheers!

**Proost!**
[prōst!]

Let's drink to ...!

**Laten we drinken op ...!**
[latən we 'drinkən ɔp ... !]

To our success!

**Op ons succes!**
[ɔp ɔns suk'sɛs!]

To your success!

**Op uw succes!**
[ɔp uw suk'sɛs!]

Good luck!

**Veel succes!**
[vēl suk'sɛs!]

Have a nice day!

**Een prettige dag!**
[en 'prɛtixə dax!]

Have a good holiday!

**Een prettige vakantie!**
[en 'prɛtixə va'kantsi!]

Have a safe journey!

**Een veilige reis!**
[en 'vɛjlixə rɛjs!]

I hope you get better soon!

**Ik hoop dat u gauw weer beter bent!**
[ik hōp dat ju 'xau wēr 'betər bɛnt!]

## Socializing

| | |
|---|---|
| Why are you sad? | **Waarom zie je er zo verdrietig uit?**<br>[wā'rɔm zi je ɛr zɔ vər'dritəx œyt?] |
| Smile! Cheer up! | **Lach eens! Wees vrolijk!**<br>[lax ēns! wēs 'vrɔlək!] |
| Are you free tonight? | **Ben je vrij vanavond?**<br>[bɛn je vrɛj va'navɔnt?] |

| | |
|---|---|
| May I offer you a drink? | **Mag ik je een drankje aanbieden?**<br>[max ik je en 'drankje 'ānbidən?] |
| Would you like to dance? | **Zullen we eens dansen?**<br>[zʉlən we ēns 'dansən?] |
| Let's go to the movies. | **Laten we naar de bioscoop gaan.**<br>[latən we nār də biɔ'skōp xān] |

| | |
|---|---|
| May I invite you to ...? | **Mag ik je uitnodigen naar ...?**<br>[max ik je 'œytnɔdixən nār ...?] |
| a restaurant | **een restaurant**<br>[en rɛstɔ'ran] |
| the movies | **de bioscoop**<br>[də biɔ'skōp] |
| the theater | **het theater**<br>[hɛt te'ater] |
| go for a walk | **een wandeling**<br>[en 'wandəliŋ] |

| | |
|---|---|
| At what time? | **Hoe laat?**<br>[hu lāt?] |
| tonight | **vanavond**<br>[va'navɔnt] |
| at six | **om zes uur**<br>[ɔm zɛs ūr] |
| at seven | **om zeven uur**<br>[ɔm 'zevən ūr] |
| at eight | **om acht uur**<br>[ɔm axt ūr] |
| at nine | **om negen uur**<br>[ɔm 'nexən ūr] |

| | |
|---|---|
| Do you like it here? | **Vind u het hier leuk?**<br>[vint ju ət hir 'løk?] |
| Are you here with someone? | **Bent u hier met iemand?**<br>[bɛnt ju hir mɛt i'mant?] |
| I'm with my friend. | **Ik ben met mijn vriend.**<br>[ik bɛn mɛt mɛjn vrint] |

| | |
|---|---|
| I'm with my friends. | **Ik ben met mijn vrienden.** |
| | [ik bɛn mɛt mɛjn 'vrindən] |
| No, I'm alone. | **Nee, ik ben alleen.** |
| | [ik bɛn a'lēn] |

| | |
|---|---|
| Do you have a boyfriend? | **Heb jij een vriendje?** |
| | [hɛp jɛj en 'vrindje?] |
| I have a boyfriend. | **Ik heb een vriendje.** |
| | [ik hɛp en 'vrindje] |
| Do you have a girlfriend? | **Heb jij een vriendin?** |
| | [hɛp jɛj en vrin'din?] |
| I have a girlfriend. | **Ik heb een vriendin.** |
| | [ik hɛp en vrin'din] |

| | |
|---|---|
| Can I see you again? | **Kan ik je weer eens zien?** |
| | [kan ik je wēr ēns zin?] |
| Can I call you? | **Mag ik je opbellen?** |
| | [max ik je ɔ'bɛlən?] |
| Call me. (Give me a call.) | **Bel me op.** |
| | [bɛl mə ɔp] |
| What's your number? | **Wat is je nummer?** |
| | [wat is je 'nʉmər?] |
| I miss you. | **Ik mis je.** |
| | [ik mis je] |

| | |
|---|---|
| You have a beautiful name. | **U hebt een mooie naam.** |
| | [ju hɛpt en mōje nām] |
| I love you. | **Ik hou van jou.** |
| | [ik 'hau van 'jau] |
| Will you marry me? | **Wil je met me trouwen?** |
| | [wil je mɛt mə 'trauwən?] |
| You're kidding! | **Dat meen je niet!** |
| | [dat mēn je nit!] |
| I'm just kidding. | **Grapje.** |
| | [xrapje] |

| | |
|---|---|
| Are you serious? | **Meen je dat?** |
| | [mēn je dat?] |
| I'm serious. | **Ik meen het.** |
| | [ik mēn ət] |
| Really?! | **Heus waar?!** |
| | [høs wār?!] |
| It's unbelievable! | **Dat is ongelooflijk!** |
| | [dat is ɔnxə'lōflək!] |
| I don't believe you. | **Ik geloof je niet.** |
| | [ik xə'lōf je nit] |
| I can't. | **Ik kan niet.** |
| | [ik kan nit] |
| I don't know. | **Ik weet het niet.** |
| | [ik wēt ət nit] |
| I don't understand you. | **Ik versta u niet.** |
| | [ik vər'sta ju nit] |

Please go away.

**Ga alstublieft weg.**
[xa alstʉ'blift wɛx]

Leave me alone!

**Laat me gerust!**
[lãt mə xə'rʉst!]

I can't stand him.

**Ik kan hem niet uitstaan.**
[ik kan hɛm nit 'œʏtstãn]

You are disgusting!

**U bent een smeerlap!**
[ju bɛnt en 'smērlap!]

I'll call the police!

**Ik ga de politie bellen!**
[ik xa də pɔ'litsi 'bɛlən!]

## Sharing impressions. Emotions

I like it.
**Dat vind ik fijn.**
[dat vint ik fɛjn]

Very nice.
**Heel mooi.**
[hēl mōj]

That's great!
**Wat leuk!**
[wat 'løk!]

It's not bad.
**Dat is niet slecht.**
[dat is nit slɛxt]

I don't like it.
**Daar houd ik niet van.**
[dār 'haut ik nit van]

It's not good.
**Dat is niet goed.**
[dat is nit xut]

It's bad.
**Het is slecht.**
[hɛt is slɛxt]

It's very bad.
**Het is heel slecht.**
[hɛt is hēl slɛxt]

It's disgusting.
**Het is smerig.**
[hɛt is 'smerəx]

I'm happy.
**Ik ben blij.**
[ik bɛn blɛj]

I'm content.
**Ik ben tevreden.**
[ik bɛn təv'redən]

I'm in love.
**ik ben verliefd.**
[ik bɛn vər'lift]

I'm calm.
**Ik voel me rustig.**
[ik vul mə 'rʉstəx]

I'm bored.
**Ik verveel me.**
[ik vər'vēl mə]

I'm tired.
**Ik ben moe.**
[ik bɛn mu]

I'm sad.
**Ik ben verdrietig.**
[ik bɛn vər'dritəx]

I'm frightened.
**Ik ben bang.**
[ik bɛn baŋ]

I'm angry.
**Ik ben kwaad.**
[ik bɛn kwāt]

I'm worried.
**Ik ben bezorgd.**
[ik bɛn bə'zɔrxt]

I'm nervous.
**Ik ben zenuwachtig.**
[ik bɛn 'zenʉwaxtəx]

I'm jealous. (envious)

**Ik ben jaloers.**
[ik bɛn ja'lurs]

I'm surprised.

**Het verwondert me.**
[hɛt vər'wɔndərt mə]

I'm perplexed.

**Ik sta paf.**
[ik sta paf]

## Problems. Accidents

I've got a problem.

**Ik heb een probleem.**
[ik hɛp en prɔ'blēm]

We've got a problem.

**Wij hebben een probleem.**
[wɛj 'hɛbən en prɔ'blēm]

I'm lost.

**Ik ben de weg kwijt.**
[ik bɛn də wɛx kwɛjt]

I missed the last bus (train).

**Ik heb de laatste bus (trein) gemist.**
[ik hɛp də 'lātstə bus (trɛjn) xə'mist]

I don't have any money left.

**Ik heb geen geld meer.**
[ik hɛp xēn xɛlt mēr]

I've lost my ...

**Ik heb mijn ... verloren**
[ik hɛp mɛjn ... vər'lɔrən]

Someone stole my ...

**Iemand heeft mijn ... gestolen**
[imant hēft mɛjn ... xəs'tɔlən]

passport

**paspoort**
[paspōrt]

wallet

**portemonnee**
[pɔrtəmɔ'nē]

papers

**papieren**
[pa'pirən]

ticket

**kaartje**
[kārtjə]

money

**geld**
[xɛlt]

handbag

**tas**
[tas]

camera

**camera**
[kaməra]

laptop

**laptop**
['lɛptɔp]

tablet computer

**tablet**
[tab'lɛt]

mobile phone

**mobieltje**
[mɔ'biltjə]

Help me!

**Help!**
[hɛlp!]

What's happened?

**Wat is er aan de hand?**
[wat is ɛr ān də hant?]

fire

**brand**
[brant]

shooting
**er wordt geschoten**
[ɛr wɔrt xəs'xɔtən]

murder
**moord**
[mõrt]

explosion
**ontploffing**
[ɔntp'lɔfiŋ]

fight
**gevecht**
[xə'vɛxt]

---

Call the police!
**Bel de politie!**
[bɛl də pɔ'litsi!]

Please hurry up!
**Opschieten alstublieft!**
[ɔpsxitən alstʉ'blift!]

I'm looking for the police station.
**Ik zoek het politiebureau.**
[ik zuk ət pɔ'litsi bʉ'rɔ]

I need to make a call.
**Ik moet opbellen.**
[ik mut ɔ'bɛlən]

May I use your phone?
**Mag ik uw telefoon gebruiken?**
[max ik ʉw telə'fõn xe'brœʏkən?]

---

I've been ...
**Ik ben ...**
[ik bɛn ...]

mugged
**overvallen**
[ɔvər'valən]

robbed
**bestolen**
[bəs'tɔlən]

raped
**verkracht**
[vərk'raxt]

attacked (beaten up)
**aangevallen**
[ānxəvalən]

---

Are you all right?
**Gaat het?**
[xāt ət?]

Did you see who it was?
**Hebt u gezien wie het was?**
[hɛpt ju xə'zin wi ət was?]

Would you be able to recognize the person?
**Zou u de persoon kunnen herkennen?**
[zau ju də pɛr'sõn 'kʉnən hɛr'kɛnən?]

Are you sure?
**Bent u daar zeker van?**
[bɛnt ju dār 'zekər van?]

---

Please calm down.
**Rustig aan alstublieft.**
[rʉstəx ān alstʉ'blift]

Take it easy!
**Kalm aan!**
[kalm ān!]

Don't worry!
**Maak je geen zorgen!**
[māk je xēn 'zɔrxən!]

Everything will be fine.
**Alles komt in orde.**
[aləs kɔmt in 'ɔrdə]

Everything's all right.
**Alles is in orde.**
[aləs iz in 'ɔrdə]

Come here, please.
**Kom hier alstublieft.**
[kɔm hir alstʉ'blift]

I have some questions for you.

**Ik heb een paar vragen voor u.**
[ik hɛp en pãr 'vraxən võr ju]

Wait a moment, please.

**Een ogenblikje alstublieft.**
[en 'ɔxənblikje alstʉ'blift]

Do you have any I.D.?

**Hebt u een ID-kaart?**
[hɛpt ju en aj'di-kãrt?]

Thanks. You can leave now.

**Dank u. U mag nu vertrekken.**
[dank ju. ju max nʉ vər'trɛkən]

Hands behind your head!

**Handen achter uw hoofd!**
[handən 'axtər ʉw hõft!]

You're under arrest!

**U bent onder arrest!**
[ju bɛnt 'ɔndər a'rɛst!]

# Health problems

| | |
|---|---|
| Please help me. | **Kunt u mij helpen alstublieft?**<br>[kʉnt ju mɛj 'hɛlpən alstʉ'blift] |
| I don't feel well. | **Ik voel me niet goed.**<br>[ik vul mə nit xut] |
| My husband doesn't feel well. | **Mijn man voelt zich niet goed.**<br>[mɛjn man vult zix nit xut] |
| My son ... | **Mijn zoon ...**<br>[mɛjn zōn ...] |
| My father ... | **Mijn vader ...**<br>[mɛjn 'vadər ...] |

| | |
|---|---|
| My wife doesn't feel well. | **Mijn vrouw voelt zich niet goed.**<br>[mɛjn 'vrau vult zix nit xut] |
| My daughter ... | **Mijn dochter ...**<br>[mɛjn 'dɔxtər ...] |
| My mother ... | **Mijn moeder ...**<br>[mɛjn 'mudər ...] |

| | |
|---|---|
| I've got a ... | **Ik heb ...**<br>[ik hɛp ...] |
| headache | **hoofdpijn**<br>[hōftpɛjn] |
| sore throat | **keelpijn**<br>[kēlpɛjn] |
| stomach ache | **maagpijn**<br>[māxpɛjn] |
| toothache | **tandpijn**<br>[tantpɛjn] |

| | |
|---|---|
| I feel dizzy. | **Ik voel me duizelig.**<br>[ik vul mə 'dœyzələx] |
| He has a fever. | **Hij heeft koorts.**<br>[hɛj hēft kōrts] |
| She has a fever. | **Zij heeft koorts.**<br>[zɛj hēft kōrts] |
| I can't breathe. | **Ik heb moeite met ademen.**<br>[ik hɛp 'mujtə mɛt 'adəmən] |

| | |
|---|---|
| I'm short of breath. | **Ik ben kortademig.**<br>[ik bɛn kɔ'rtadəməx] |
| I am asthmatic. | **Ik ben astmatisch.**<br>[ik bɛn astm'atis] |
| I am diabetic. | **Ik ben diabeet.**<br>[ik bɛn 'diabēt] |

| | |
|---|---|
| I can't sleep. | **Ik kan niet slapen.** |
| | [ik kan nit 'slapən] |
| food poisoning | **voedselvergiftiging** |
| | [vutsəl·vər'xiftəxiŋ] |

| | |
|---|---|
| It hurts here. | **Het doet hier pijn.** |
| | [hɛt dut hir pɛjn] |
| Help me! | **Help!** |
| | [hɛlp!] |
| I am here! | **Ik ben hier!** |
| | [ik bɛn hir!] |
| We are here! | **Wij zijn hier!** |
| | [wɛj zɛjn hir!] |
| Get me out of here! | **Kom mij halen!** |
| | [kɔm mɛj 'halən!] |
| I need a doctor. | **Ik heb een dokter nodig.** |
| | [ik hɛp en 'dɔktər 'nɔdəx] |
| I can't move. | **Ik kan me niet bewegen.** |
| | [ik kan mə nit bə'wexən] |
| I can't move my legs. | **Ik kan mijn benen niet bewegen.** |
| | [ik kan mɛjn 'benən nit bə'wexən] |

| | |
|---|---|
| I have a wound. | **Ik heb een wond.** |
| | [ik hɛp en wɔnt] |
| Is it serious? | **Is het erg?** |
| | [iz ət ɛrx?] |
| My documents are in my pocket. | **Mijn documenten zijn in mijn zak.** |
| | [mɛjn dɔkʉ'mɛntən zɛjn in mɛjn zak] |
| Calm down! | **Rustig maar!** |
| | [rʉstəx mār!] |
| May I use your phone? | **Mag ik uw telefoon gebruiken?** |
| | [max ik ʉw telə'fōn xə'brœykən?] |

| | |
|---|---|
| Call an ambulance! | **Bel een ambulance!** |
| | [bɛl en ambʉ'lansə!] |
| It's urgent! | **Het is dringend!** |
| | [hɛt is 'driŋənt!] |
| It's an emergency! | **Het is een noodgeval!** |
| | [hɛt is en 'nōtxəval!] |
| Please hurry up! | **Opschieten alstublieft!** |
| | [ɔpsxitən alstʉ'blift!] |
| Would you please call a doctor? | **Kunt u alstublieft een dokter bellen?** |
| | [kʉnt ju alstʉ'blift en 'dɔktər 'bɛlən?] |
| Where is the hospital? | **Waar is het ziekenhuis?** |
| | [wār iz ət 'zikənhœys?] |

| | |
|---|---|
| How are you feeling? | **Hoe voelt u zich?** |
| | [hu vult ju zix?] |
| Are you all right? | **Hoe gaat het?** |
| | [hu xāt ət?] |
| What's happened? | **Wat is er gebeurd?** |
| | [wat is ɛr xə'børt?] |

I feel better now.

**Ik voel me nu wat beter.**
[ik vul mə nʉ wat 'betər]

It's OK.

**Het is okay.**
[hɛt is ɔ'kɛj]

It's all right.

**Het gaat beter.**
[hɛt xāt 'betər]

## At the pharmacy

pharmacy (drugstore)

**apotheek**
[apɔ'tēk]

24-hour pharmacy

**dag en nacht apotheek**
[dax en naxt apɔ'tēk]

Where is the closest pharmacy?

**Waar is de meest nabij gelegen apotheek?**
[wār is də mēst na'bɛj xə'lexən apɔ'tēk?]

Is it open now?

**Is hij nu open?**
[is hɛj nʉ 'ɔpən?]

At what time does it open?

**Hoe laat gaat hij open?**
[hu lāt xāt hɛj 'ɔpən?]

At what time does it close?

**Hoe laat sluit hij?**
[hu lāt slœyt hɛj?]

Is it far?

**Is het ver?**
[iz ət vɛr?]

Can I get there on foot?

**Kan ik er lopend naar toe?**
[kan ik ɛr 'lopənt nār tu?]

Can you show me on the map?

**Kunt u het op de plattegrond aanwijzen?**
[kʉnt ju ət ɔp də platə'xrɔnt 'ānwɛjzən?]

Please give me something for …

**Geef mij alstublieft iets voor …**
[xēf mɛj alstʉ'blift its vōr …]

a headache

**hoofdpijn**
[hõftpɛjn]

a cough

**hoest**
[hust]

a cold

**verkoudheid**
[vər'kauthɛjt]

the flu

**de griep**
[də xrip]

a fever

**koorts**
[kõrts]

a stomach ache

**maagpijn**
[māxpɛjn]

nausea

**misselijkheid**
['misələkhɛjt]

diarrhea

**diarree**
[dia'rē]

| | |
|---|---|
| constipation | **constipatie**<br>[kɔnsti'patsi] |
| pain in the back | **rugpijn**<br>[rʏxpɛjn] |
| chest pain | **pijn in mijn borst**<br>[pɛjn in mɛjn bɔrst] |
| side stitch | **steek in de zij**<br>[stēk in də zɛj] |
| abdominal pain | **pijn in mijn onderbuik**<br>[pɛjn in mɛjn 'ɔndərbœʏk] |

| | |
|---|---|
| pill | **pil**<br>[pil] |
| ointment, cream | **zalf, crème**<br>[zalf, krɛ:m] |
| syrup | **stroop**<br>[strōp] |
| spray | **verstuiver**<br>[vərstœʏvər] |
| drops | **druppels**<br>[drʏpəls] |

| | |
|---|---|
| You need to go to the hospital. | **U moet naar het ziekenhuis.**<br>[ju mut nār ət 'zikənhœʏs] |
| health insurance | **ziektekostenverzekering**<br>[ziktəkɔstən·vər'zekəriŋ] |
| prescription | **voorschrift**<br>[vōrsxrift] |
| insect repellant | **anti-insecten middel**<br>[anti-in'sɛktən 'midəl] |
| Band Aid | **pleister**<br>['plɛjstər] |

# The bare minimum

| | |
|---|---|
| Excuse me, ... | **Pardon, ...**<br>[par'dɔn, ...] |
| Hello. | **Hallo.**<br>[halɔ] |
| Thank you. | **Bedankt.**<br>[bə'dankt] |
| Good bye. | **Tot ziens.**<br>[tɔt zins] |
| Yes. | **Ja.**<br>[ja] |
| No. | **Nee.**<br>[nē] |
| I don't know. | **Ik weet het niet.**<br>[ik wēt ət nit] |
| Where? | Where to? | When? | **Waar? | Waarheen? | Wanneer?**<br>[wār? | wār'hēn? | wa'nēr?] |

| | |
|---|---|
| I need ... | **Ik heb ... nodig**<br>[ik hɛp ... 'nɔdəx] |
| I want ... | **Ik wil ...**<br>[ik wil ...] |
| Do you have ...? | **Hebt u ...?**<br>[hɛpt ju ...?] |
| Is there a ... here? | **Is hier een ...?**<br>[is hir en ...?] |
| May I ...? | **Mag ik ...?**<br>[max ik ...?] |
| ..., please (polite request) | **... alstublieft**<br>[... alstʉ'blift] |

| | |
|---|---|
| I'm looking for ... | **Ik zoek ...**<br>[ik zuk ...] |
| restroom | **toilet**<br>[twa'lɛt] |
| ATM | **geldautomaat**<br>[xɛlt·autɔ'māt] |
| pharmacy (drugstore) | **apotheek**<br>[apɔ'tēk] |
| hospital | **ziekenhuis**<br>[zikənhœʏs] |
| police station | **politiebureau**<br>[pɔ\'litsi bʉ\'rɔ] |
| subway | **metro**<br>['metrɔ] |

| | |
|---|---|
| taxi | **taxi** |
| | [taksi] |
| train station | **station** |
| | [sta'tsjɔn] |

| | |
|---|---|
| My name is ... | **Ik heet ...** |
| | [ik hēt ...] |
| What's your name? | **Hoe heet u?** |
| | [hu hēt ju?] |
| Could you please help me? | **Kunt u me helpen alstublieft?** |
| | [kʊnt ju mə 'hɛlpən alstʉ'blift?] |
| I've got a problem. | **Ik heb een probleem.** |
| | [ik hɛp en prɔ'blēm] |
| I don't feel well. | **Ik voel me niet goed.** |
| | [ik vul mə nit xut] |
| Call an ambulance! | **Bel een ambulance!** |
| | [bɛl en ambʉ'lansə!] |
| May I make a call? | **Mag ik opbellen?** |
| | [max ik ɔ'bɛlən?] |

| | |
|---|---|
| I'm sorry. | **Sorry.** |
| | ['sɔri] |
| You're welcome. | **Graag gedaan.** |
| | [xrãx xə'dãn] |

| | |
|---|---|
| I, me | **Ik, mij** |
| | [ik, mɛj] |
| you (inform.) | **jij** |
| | [jɛj] |
| he | **hij** |
| | [hɛj] |
| she | **zij** |
| | [zɛj] |
| they (masc.) | **zij** |
| | [zɛj] |
| they (fem.) | **zij** |
| | [zɛj] |
| we | **wij** |
| | [wɛj] |
| you (pl) | **jullie** |
| | ['juli] |
| you (sg, form.) | **u** |
| | [ju] |

| | |
|---|---|
| ENTRANCE | **INGANG** |
| | [inxaŋ] |
| EXIT | **UITGANG** |
| | [œʏtxaŋ] |
| OUT OF ORDER | **BUITEN GEBRUIK** |
| | [bœʏtən xə'brœʏk] |
| CLOSED | **GESLOTEN** |
| | [xə'slɔtən] |

| | |
|---|---|
| OPEN | **OPEN**<br>['ɔpən] |
| FOR WOMEN | **DAMES**<br>[daməs] |
| FOR MEN | **HEREN**<br>['herən] |

# TOPICAL VOCABULARY

This section contains more than 3,000 of the most important words.
The dictionary will provide invaluable assistance while traveling abroad, because frequently individual words are enough for you to be understood.
The dictionary includes a convenient transcription of each foreign word

T&P Books Publishing

# VOCABULARY
# CONTENTS

T&P Books Publishing

BOOKS

# BASIC CONCEPTS

**T&P Books Publishing**

## 1. Pronouns

| | | |
|---|---|---|
| I, me | **ik** | [ik] |
| you | **jij, je** | [jɛj], [jə] |
| | | |
| he | **hij** | [hɛj] |
| she | **zij, ze** | [zɛj], [zə] |
| it | **het** | [ət] |
| | | |
| we | **wij, we** | [wɛj], [wə] |
| you (to a group) | **jullie** | ['juli] |
| they | **zij, ze** | [zɛj], [zə] |

## 2. Greetings. Salutations

| | | |
|---|---|---|
| Hello! (fam.) | **Hallo! Dag!** | [ha'lɔ dax] |
| Hello! (form.) | **Hallo!** | [ha'lɔ] |
| Good morning! | **Goedemorgen!** | ['xudə·'mɔrxən] |
| Good afternoon! | **Goedemiddag!** | ['xudə·'midax] |
| Good evening! | **Goedenavond!** | ['xudən·'avɔnt] |
| | | |
| to say hello | **gedag zeggen** | [xe'dax 'zexən] |
| Hi! (hello) | **Hoi!** | [hɔj] |
| greeting (n) | **groeten (het)** | ['xrutən] |
| to greet (vt) | **verwelkomen** | [vər'wɛlkɔmən] |
| How are you? | **Hoe gaat het?** | [hu xāt ət] |
| What's new? | **Is er nog nieuws?** | [is ɛr nɔx 'nius] |
| | | |
| Goodbye! | **Tot ziens!** | [tɔt 'tsins] |
| Bye! | **Doei!** | ['dui] |
| See you soon! | **Tot snel!** | [tɔt snɛl] |
| Farewell! | **Vaarwel!** | [vār'wɛl] |
| to say goodbye | **afscheid nemen** | ['afsxɛjt 'nemən] |
| So long! | **Tot kijk!** | [tɔt kɛjk] |
| | | |
| Thank you! | **Dank u!** | [dank ju] |
| Thank you very much! | **Dank u wel!** | [dank ju wɛl] |
| You're welcome. | **Graag gedaan.** | [xrāx xə'dān] |
| Don't mention it. | **Geen dank.** | [xēn dank] |
| It was nothing. | **Geen moeite.** | [xēn 'mujtə] |
| | | |
| Excuse me! | **Excuseer me, ...** | [ɛkskʉ'zēr mə] |
| to excuse (forgive) | **excuseren** | [ɛkskʉ'zerən] |
| to apologize (vi) | **zich verontschuldigen** | [zih vərɔnt'sxʉldəxən] |

| My apologies | Mijn excuses | [mɛjn ɛks'kʉzəs] |
| I'm sorry! | Het spijt me! | [ət spɛjt mə] |
| to forgive (vt) | vergeven | [vər'xevən] |
| It's okay! (that's all right) | Maakt niet uit! | [mãk nit œyt] |
| please (adv) | alsjeblieft | [alstʉ'blift] |
| | | |
| Don't forget! | Vergeet het niet! | [vər'xēt ət nit] |
| Certainly! | Natuurlijk! | [na'tūrlək] |
| Of course not! | Natuurlijk niet! | [na'tūrlək nit] |
| Okay! (I agree) | Akkoord! | [a'kõrt] |
| That's enough! | Zo is het genoeg! | [zɔ is ət xə'nux] |

## 3. Questions

| Who? | Wie? | [wi] |
| What? | Wat? | [wat] |
| Where? (at, in) | Waar? | [wãr] |
| Where (to)? | Waarheen? | [wãr'hēn] |
| From where? | Waarvandaan? | [ʋãr·van'dãn] |
| When? | Wanneer? | [wa'nēr] |
| Why? (What for?) | Waarom? | [wãr'ɔm] |
| Why? (~ are you crying?) | Waarom? | [wãr'ɔm] |
| | | |
| What for? | Waarvoor dan ook? | [wãr'võr dan 'õk] |
| How? (in what way) | Hoe? | [hu] |
| What? (What kind of …?) | Wat voor …? | [wat vɔr] |
| Which? | Welk? | [wɛlk] |
| | | |
| To whom? | Aan wie? | [ãn wi] |
| About whom? | Over wie? | ['ɔvər wi] |
| About what? | Waarover? | [wãr'ɔvər] |
| With whom? | Met wie? | [mɛt 'wi] |
| | | |
| How many? How much? | Hoeveel? | [hu'vēl] |
| Whose? | Van wie? | [van 'wi] |

## 4. Prepositions

| with (accompanied by) | met | [mɛt] |
| without | zonder | ['zɔndər] |
| to (indicating direction) | naar | [nãr] |
| about (talking ~ …) | over | ['ɔvər] |
| before (in time) | voor | [võr] |
| in front of … | voor | [võr] |
| | | |
| under (beneath, below) | onder | ['ɔndər] |
| above (over) | boven | ['bɔvən] |
| on (atop) | op | [ɔp] |

| from (off, out of) | van | [van] |
| of (made from) | van | [van] |

| in (e.g., ~ ten minutes) | over | ['ɔvər] |
| over (across the top of) | over | ['ɔvər] |

## 5. Function words. Adverbs. Part 1

| Where? (at, in) | Waar? | [wār] |
| here (adv) | hier | [hir] |
| there (adv) | daar | [dār] |

| somewhere (to be) | ergens | ['ɛrxəns] |
| nowhere (not anywhere) | nergens | ['nɛrxəns] |

| by (near, beside) | bij ... | [bɛj] |
| by the window | bij het raam | [bɛj het 'rām] |

| Where (to)? | Waarheen? | [wār'hēn] |
| here (e.g., come ~!) | hierheen | [hir'hēn] |
| there (e.g., to go ~) | daarheen | [dār'hēn] |
| from here (adv) | hiervandaan | [hirvan'dān] |
| from there (adv) | daarvandaan | [darvan'dān] |

| close (adv) | dichtbij | [dix'bɛj] |
| far (adv) | ver | [vɛr] |

| near (e.g., ~ Paris) | in de buurt | [in də būrt] |
| nearby (adv) | dichtbij | [dix'bɛj] |
| not far (adv) | niet ver | [nit vɛr] |

| left (adj) | linker | ['linkər] |
| on the left | links | [links] |
| to the left | linksaf, naar links | ['linksaf], [nār 'links] |

| right (adj) | rechter | ['rɛxtər] |
| on the right | rechts | [rɛxts] |
| to the right | rechtsaf, naar rechts | ['rɛxtsaf], [nār 'rɛxts] |

| in front (adv) | vooraan | [võ'rān] |
| front (as adj) | voorste | ['võrstə] |
| ahead (the kids ran ~) | vooruit | [võr'œʏt] |

| behind (adv) | achter | ['axtər] |
| from behind | van achteren | [van 'axtərən] |
| back (towards the rear) | achteruit | ['axtərœʏt] |

| middle | midden (het) | ['midən] |
| in the middle | in het midden | [in ət 'midən] |
| at the side | opzij | [ɔp'sɛj] |

| everywhere (adv) | overal | [ɔvəˈral] |
| around (in all directions) | omheen | [ɔmˈhēn] |

| from inside | binnenuit | [ˈbinənœyt] |
| somewhere (to go) | naar ergens | [nǎr ˈɛrxəns] |
| straight (directly) | rechtdoor | [rɛxˈdōr] |
| back (e.g., come ~) | terug | [teˈrʉx] |

| from anywhere | ergens vandaan | [ˈɛrxəns vanˈdān] |
| from somewhere | ergens vandaan | [ˈɛrxəns vanˈdān] |

| firstly (adv) | ten eerste | [tən ˈērstə] |
| secondly (adv) | ten tweede | [tən ˈtwēdə] |
| thirdly (adv) | ten derde | [tən ˈdɛrdə] |

| suddenly (adv) | plotseling | [ˈplɔtseliŋ] |
| at first (in the beginning) | in het begin | [in ət bəˈxin] |
| for the first time | voor de eerste keer | [vōr də ˈērstə kēr] |
| long before ... | lang voor ... | [laŋ vōr] |
| anew (over again) | opnieuw | [ɔpˈniu] |
| for good (adv) | voor eeuwig | [vōr ˈēwəx] |

| never (adv) | nooit | [nōjt] |
| again (adv) | weer | [wēr] |
| now (adv) | nu | [nʉ] |
| often (adv) | vaak | [vāk] |
| then (adv) | toen | [tun] |
| urgently (quickly) | urgent | [jurxənt] |
| usually (adv) | meestal | [ˈmēstal] |

| by the way, ... | trouwens, ... | [ˈtrauwəns] |
| possible (that is ~) | mogelijk | [ˈmɔxələk] |
| probably (adv) | waarschijnlijk | [wǎrˈsxɛjnlək] |
| maybe (adv) | misschien | [misˈxin] |
| besides ... | trouwens | [ˈtrauwəns] |
| that's why ... | daarom ... | [dǎˈrɔm] |
| in spite of ... | in weerwil van ... | [in ˈwērwil van] |
| thanks to ... | dankzij ... | [dankˈzɛj] |

| what (pron.) | wat | [wat] |
| that (conj.) | dat | [dat] |
| something | iets | [its] |
| anything (something) | iets | [its] |
| nothing | niets | [nits] |

| who (pron.) | wie | [wi] |
| someone | iemand | [ˈimant] |
| somebody | iemand | [ˈimant] |

| nobody | niemand | [ˈnimant] |
| nowhere (a voyage to ~) | nergens | [ˈnɛrxəns] |
| nobody's | niemands | [ˈnimants] |

| somebody's | iemands | ['imants] |
| so (I'm ~ glad) | zo | [zɔ] |
| also (as well) | ook | [ōk] |
| too (as well) | alsook | [al'sōk] |

## 6. Function words. Adverbs. Part 2

| Why? | Waarom? | [wār'ɔm] |
| for some reason | om een bepaalde reden | [ɔm en be'pāldə 'redən] |
| because ... | omdat ... | [ɔm'dat] |
| for some purpose | voor een bepaald doel | [vōr en be'pālt dul] |

| and | en | [en] |
| or | of | [ɔf] |
| but | maar | [mār] |
| for (e.g., ~ me) | voor | [vōr] |

| too (~ many people) | te | [te] |
| only (exclusively) | alleen | [a'lēn] |
| exactly (adv) | precies | [prə'sis] |
| about (more or less) | ongeveer | [ɔnxə'vēr] |

| approximately (adv) | ongeveer | [ɔnxə'vēr] |
| approximate (adj) | bij benadering | [bɛj bə'nadəriŋ] |
| almost (adv) | bijna | ['bɛjna] |
| the rest | rest (de) | [rɛst] |

| the other (second) | de andere | [də 'andərə] |
| other (different) | ander | ['andər] |
| each (adj) | elk | [ɛlk] |
| any (no matter which) | om het even welk | [ɔm ət ɛvən wɛlk] |
| many, much (a lot of) | veel | [vēl] |
| many people | veel mensen | [vēl 'mɛnsən] |
| all (everyone) | iedereen | [idə'rēn] |

| in return for ... | in ruil voor ... | [in 'rœyl vōr] |
| in exchange (adv) | in ruil | [in 'rœyl] |
| by hand (made) | met de hand | [mɛt də 'hant] |
| hardly (negative opinion) | onwaarschijnlijk | [ɔnwār'sxɛjnlək] |

| probably (adv) | waarschijnlijk | [wār'sxɛjnlək] |
| on purpose (intentionally) | met opzet | [mɛt 'ɔpzət] |
| by accident (adv) | toevallig | [tu'valəx] |

| very (adv) | zeer | [zēr] |
| for example (adv) | bijvoorbeeld | [bɛj'vōrbēlt] |
| between | tussen | ['tʉsən] |
| among | tussen | ['tʉsən] |
| so much (such a lot) | zoveel | [zɔ'vēl] |
| especially (adv) | vooral | [vō'ral] |

# NUMBERS.
# MISCELLANEOUS

**T&P Books Publishing**

# 7. Cardinal numbers. Part 1

| | | |
|---|---|---|
| 0 zero | nul | [nʉl] |
| 1 one | een | [en] |
| 2 two | twee | [twē] |
| 3 three | drie | [dri] |
| 4 four | vier | [vir] |
| | | |
| 5 five | vijf | [vɛjf] |
| 6 six | zes | [zɛs] |
| 7 seven | zeven | ['zevən] |
| 8 eight | acht | [axt] |
| 9 nine | negen | ['nexən] |
| | | |
| 10 ten | tien | [tin] |
| 11 eleven | elf | [ɛlf] |
| 12 twelve | twaalf | [twālf] |
| 13 thirteen | dertien | ['dɛrtin] |
| 14 fourteen | veertien | ['vērtin] |
| | | |
| 15 fifteen | vijftien | ['vɛjftin] |
| 16 sixteen | zestien | ['zɛstin] |
| 17 seventeen | zeventien | ['zevəntin] |
| 18 eighteen | achttien | ['axtin] |
| 19 nineteen | negentien | ['nexəntin] |
| | | |
| 20 twenty | twintig | ['twintəx] |
| 21 twenty-one | eenentwintig | ['ēnən·'twintəx] |
| 22 twenty-two | tweeëntwintig | ['twēɛn·'twintəx] |
| 23 twenty-three | drieëntwintig | ['driɛn·'twintəx] |
| | | |
| 30 thirty | dertig | ['dɛrtəx] |
| 31 thirty-one | eenendertig | ['ēnən·'dɛrtəx] |
| 32 thirty-two | tweeëndertig | ['twēɛn·'dɛrtəx] |
| 33 thirty-three | drieëndertig | ['driɛn·'dɛrtəx] |
| | | |
| 40 forty | veertig | ['vērtəx] |
| 41 forty-one | eenenveertig | ['ēnən·'vertəx] |
| 42 forty-two | tweeënveertig | ['twēɛn·'vertəx] |
| 43 forty-three | drieënveertig | ['driɛn·'vērtəx] |
| | | |
| 50 fifty | vijftig | ['vɛjftəx] |
| 51 fifty-one | eenenvijftig | ['ēnən·'vɛjftəx] |
| 52 fifty-two | tweeënvijftig | ['twēɛn·'vɛjftəx] |
| 53 fifty-three | drieënvijftig | ['driɛn·'vɛjftəx] |
| 60 sixty | zestig | ['zɛstəx] |

| 61 sixty-one | eenenzestig | ['ēnən·'zɛstəx] |
| 62 sixty-two | tweeènzestig | ['twēɛn·'zɛstəx] |
| 63 sixty-three | drieènzestig | ['driɛn·'zɛstəx] |
| | | |
| 70 seventy | zeventig | ['zevəntəx] |
| 71 seventy-one | eenenzeventig | ['ēnən·'zevəntəx] |
| 72 seventy-two | tweeènzeventig | ['twēɛn·'zevəntəx] |
| 73 seventy-three | drieènzeventig | ['driɛn·'zevəntəx] |
| | | |
| 80 eighty | tachtig | ['tahtəx] |
| 81 eighty-one | eenentachtig | ['ēnən·'tahtəx] |
| 82 eighty-two | tweeèntachtig | ['twēɛn·'tahtəx] |
| 83 eighty-three | drieèntachtig | ['driɛn·'taxtəx] |
| | | |
| 90 ninety | negentig | ['nexəntəx] |
| 91 ninety-one | eenennegentig | ['ēnən·'nexəntəx] |
| 92 ninety-two | tweeènnegentig | ['twēɛn·'nexəntəx] |
| 93 ninety-three | drieènnegentig | ['driɛn·'nexəntəx] |

## 8. Cardinal numbers. Part 2

| 100 one hundred | honderd | ['hɔndərt] |
| 200 two hundred | tweehonderd | [twē·'hɔndərt] |
| 300 three hundred | driehonderd | [dri·'hɔndərt] |
| 400 four hundred | vierhonderd | [vir·'hɔndərt] |
| 500 five hundred | vijfhonderd | [vɛjf·'hɔndərt] |
| | | |
| 600 six hundred | zeshonderd | [zɛs·'hɔndərt] |
| 700 seven hundred | zevenhonderd | ['zevən·'hɔndərt] |
| 800 eight hundred | achthonderd | [axt·'hɔndərt] |
| 900 nine hundred | negenhonderd | ['nexən·'hɔndərt] |
| | | |
| 1000 one thousand | duizend | ['dœyzənt] |
| 2000 two thousand | tweeduizend | [twē·'dœyzənt] |
| 3000 three thousand | drieduizend | [dri·'dœyzənt] |
| 10000 ten thousand | tienduizend | [tin·'dœyzənt] |
| one hundred thousand | honderdduizend | ['hɔndərt·'dœyzənt] |
| million | miljoen (het) | [mi'ljun] |
| billion | miljard (het) | [mi'ljart] |

## 9. Ordinal numbers

| first (adj) | eerste | ['ērstə] |
| second (adj) | tweede | ['twēdə] |
| third (adj) | derde | ['dɛrdə] |
| fourth (adj) | vierde | ['virdə] |
| fifth (adj) | vijfde | ['vɛjfdə] |
| sixth (adj) | zesde | ['zɛsdə] |

| seventh (adj) | zevende | ['zevəndə] |
| eighth (adj) | achtste | ['axtstə] |
| ninth (adj) | negende | ['nexəndə] |
| tenth (adj) | tiende | ['tində] |

T&P BOOKS

# COLOURS. UNITS OF MEASUREMENT

T&P Books Publishing

## 10. Colors

| | | |
|---|---|---|
| color | **kleur (de)** | ['klør] |
| shade (tint) | **tint (de)** | [tint] |
| hue | **kleurnuance (de)** | ['klør·nʉ'waŋsə] |
| rainbow | **regenboog (de)** | ['rexən·bõx] |
| white (adj) | **wit** | [wit] |
| black (adj) | **zwart** | [zwart] |
| gray (adj) | **grijs** | [xrɛjs] |
| green (adj) | **groen** | [xrun] |
| yellow (adj) | **geel** | [xēl] |
| red (adj) | **rood** | [rõt] |
| blue (adj) | **blauw** | ['blau] |
| light blue (adj) | **lichtblauw** | ['lixt·blau] |
| pink (adj) | **roze** | ['rɔzə] |
| orange (adj) | **oranje** | [ɔ'ranjə] |
| violet (adj) | **violet** | [viɔ'lɛt] |
| brown (adj) | **bruin** | ['brœyn] |
| golden (adj) | **goud** | ['xaut] |
| silvery (adj) | **zilverkleurig** | ['zilvər·'klørəx] |
| beige (adj) | **beige** | ['bɛ:ʒ] |
| cream (adj) | **roomkleurig** | ['rõm·'klørix] |
| turquoise (adj) | **turkoois** | [tʉrk'was] |
| cherry red (adj) | **kersrood** | ['kɛrs·rõt] |
| lilac (adj) | **lila** | ['lila] |
| crimson (adj) | **karmijnrood** | ['karmɛjn·'rõt] |
| light (adj) | **licht** | [lixt] |
| dark (adj) | **donker** | ['dɔnkər] |
| bright, vivid (adj) | **fel** | [fel] |
| colored (pencils) | **kleur-, kleurig** | ['klør], ['klørəx] |
| color (e.g., ~ film) | **kleuren-** | ['klørən] |
| black-and-white (adj) | **zwart-wit** | [zwart-wit] |
| plain (one-colored) | **eenkleurig** | [ēn'klørəx] |
| multicolored (adj) | **veelkleurig** | [vēl'klørəx] |

## 11. Units of measurement

| | | |
|---|---|---|
| weight | **gewicht (het)** | [xə'wixt] |
| length | **lengte (de)** | ['lɛŋtə] |

| width | breedte (de) | ['brētə] |
| height | hoogte (de) | ['hōxtə] |
| depth | diepte (de) | ['diptə] |
| volume | volume (het) | [vɔ'lʉmə] |
| area | oppervlakte (de) | ['ɔpərvlaktə] |

| gram | gram (het) | [xram] |
| milligram | milligram (het) | ['milixram] |
| kilogram | kilogram (het) | [kilɔxram] |
| ton | ton (de) | [tɔn] |
| pound | pond (het) | [pɔnt] |
| ounce | ons (het) | [ɔns] |

| meter | meter (de) | ['metər] |
| millimeter | millimeter (de) | ['milimetər] |
| centimeter | centimeter (de) | ['sɛnti'metər] |
| kilometer | kilometer (de) | [kilɔmetər] |
| mile | mijl (de) | [mɛjl] |

| inch | duim (de) | ['dœʏm] |
| foot | voet (de) | [vut] |
| yard | yard (de) | [jart] |

| square meter | vierkante meter (de) | ['virkantə 'metər] |
| hectare | hectare (de) | [hɛk'tarə] |
| liter | liter (de) | ['litər] |
| degree | graad (de) | [xrāt] |
| volt | volt (de) | [vɔlt] |
| ampere | ampère (de) | [am'pɛrə] |
| horsepower | paardenkracht (de) | ['pārdən·kraxt] |

| quantity | hoeveelheid (de) | [hu'vēlhɛjt] |
| a little bit of … | een beetje … | [en 'bētʃə] |
| half | helft (de) | [hɛlft] |
| dozen | dozijn (het) | [do'zɛjn] |
| piece (item) | stuk (het) | [stʉk] |

| size | afmeting (de) | ['afmetiŋ] |
| scale (map ~) | schaal (de) | [sxāl] |

| minimal (adj) | minimaal | [mini'māl] |
| the smallest (adj) | minste | ['minstə] |
| medium (adj) | medium | ['medijum] |
| maximal (adj) | maximaal | [maksi'māl] |
| the largest (adj) | grootste | ['xrōtstə] |

## 12. Containers

| canning jar (glass ~) | glazen pot (de) | ['xlazən pɔt] |
| can | blik (het) | [blik] |

| | | |
|---|---|---|
| bucket | **emmer (de)** | ['ɛmər] |
| barrel | **ton (de)** | [tɔn] |
| | | |
| wash basin (e.g., plastic ~) | **ronde waterbak (de)** | ['watər·bak] |
| tank (100L water ~) | **tank (de)** | [tank] |
| hip flask | **heupfles (de)** | ['høp·flɛs] |
| jerrycan | **jerrycan (de)** | ['dʒɛrikən] |
| tank (e.g., tank car) | **tank (de)** | [tank] |
| | | |
| mug | **beker (de)** | ['bekər] |
| cup (of coffee, etc.) | **kopje (het)** | ['kɔpjə] |
| saucer | **schoteltje (het)** | ['sxɔteltʃə] |
| glass (tumbler) | **glas (het)** | [xlas] |
| wine glass | **wijnglas (het)** | ['wɛjn·xlas] |
| stock pot (soup pot) | **pan (de)** | [pan] |
| | | |
| bottle (~ of wine) | **fles (de)** | [fles] |
| neck (of the bottle, etc.) | **flessenhals (de)** | ['flesən·hals] |
| | | |
| carafe (decanter) | **karaf (de)** | [ka'raf] |
| pitcher | **kruik (de)** | ['krœʏk] |
| vessel (container) | **vat (het)** | [vat] |
| pot (crock, stoneware ~) | **pot (de)** | [pɔt] |
| vase | **vaas (de)** | [vãs] |
| | | |
| bottle (perfume ~) | **flacon (de)** | [fla'kɔn] |
| vial, small bottle | **flesje (het)** | ['fleɕə] |
| tube (of toothpaste) | **tube (de)** | ['tʉbə] |
| | | |
| sack (bag) | **zak (de)** | [zak] |
| bag (paper ~, plastic ~) | **tasje (het)** | ['taɕə] |
| pack (of cigarettes, etc.) | **pakje (het)** | ['pakjə] |
| | | |
| box (e.g., shoebox) | **doos (de)** | [dõs] |
| crate | **kist (de)** | [kist] |
| basket | **mand (de)** | [mant] |

# MAIN VERBS

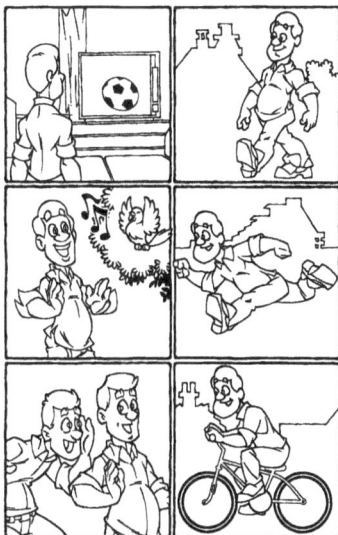

T&P Books Publishing

| | | |
|---|---|---|
| to advise (vt) | adviseren | [atvi'zirən] |
| to agree (say yes) | instemmen | ['instɛmən] |
| to answer (vi, vt) | antwoorden | ['antwõrdən] |
| to apologize (vi) | zich verontschuldigen | [zih vərɔnt'sxʉldəxən] |
| to arrive (vi) | aankomen | ['ānkɔmən] |
| | | |
| to ask (~ oneself) | vragen | ['vraxən] |
| to ask (~ sb to do sth) | verzoeken | [vər'zukən] |
| to be (vi) | zijn | [zɛjn] |
| | | |
| to be afraid | bang zijn | ['baŋ zɛjn] |
| to be hungry | honger hebben | ['hɔŋər 'hɛbən] |
| to be interested in ... | zich interesseren voor ... | [zix interə'serən võr] |
| to be needed | nodig zijn | ['nɔdəx zɛjn] |
| to be surprised | verbaasd zijn | [vər'bāst zɛjn] |
| | | |
| to be thirsty | dorst hebben | [dɔrst 'hɛbən] |
| to begin (vt) | beginnen | [bə'xinən] |
| to belong to ... | toebehoren aan ... | ['tubəhɔrən ān] |
| | | |
| to boast (vi) | opscheppen | ['ɔpsxepən] |
| to break (split into pieces) | breken | ['brekən] |
| | | |
| to call (~ for help) | roepen | ['rupən] |
| can (v aux) | kunnen | ['kʉnən] |
| to catch (vt) | vangen | ['vaŋən] |
| | | |
| to change (vt) | veranderen | [və'randərən] |
| to choose (select) | kiezen | ['kizən] |
| | | |
| to come down (the stairs) | afdalen | ['afdalən] |
| to compare (vt) | vergelijken | [vɛrxə'lɛjkən] |
| to complain (vi, vt) | klagen | ['klaxən] |
| to confuse (mix up) | verwarren | [vər'warən] |
| | | |
| to continue (vt) | vervolgen | [vər'vɔlxən] |
| to control (vt) | controleren | [kɔntrɔ'lerən] |
| | | |
| to cook (dinner) | bereiden | [bə'rɛjdən] |
| to cost (vt) | kosten | ['kɔstən] |
| to count (add up) | tellen | ['tɛlən] |
| to count on ... | rekenen op ... | ['rekənən ɔp] |
| to create (vt) | creëren | [kre'jerən] |
| to cry (weep) | huilen | ['hœvlən] |

## 14. The most important verbs. Part 2

| | | |
|---|---|---|
| to deceive (vi, vt) | **bedriegen** | [bə'drixən] |
| to decorate (tree, street) | **versieren** | [vər'sirən] |
| to defend (a country, etc.) | **verdedigen** | [vər'dedixən] |
| to demand (request firmly) | **eisen** | ['ɛjsən] |
| to dig (vt) | **graven** | ['xravən] |
| | | |
| to discuss (vt) | **bespreken** | [bə'sprekən] |
| to do (vt) | **doen** | [dun] |
| to doubt (have doubts) | **twijfelen** | ['twɛjfelən] |
| to drop (let fall) | **laten vallen** | ['latən 'valən] |
| to enter (room, house, etc.) | **binnengaan** | ['binənxān] |
| | | |
| to excuse (forgive) | **excuseren** | [ɛkskʉ'zerən] |
| to exist (vi) | **existeren** | [ɛksis'tɛrən] |
| to expect (foresee) | **voorzien** | [vōr'zin] |
| | | |
| to explain (vt) | **verklaren** | [vər'klarən] |
| to fall (vi) | **vallen** | ['valən] |
| | | |
| to find (vt) | **vinden** | ['vindən] |
| to finish (vt) | **beëindigen** | [be'ɛjndəxən] |
| to fly (vi) | **vliegen** | ['vlixən] |
| | | |
| to follow ... (come after) | **volgen** | ['vɔlxən] |
| to forget (vi, vt) | **vergeten** | [vər'xetən] |
| | | |
| to forgive (vt) | **vergeven** | [vər'xevən] |
| to give (vt) | **geven** | ['xevən] |
| | | |
| to give a hint | **een hint geven** | [en hint 'xevən] |
| to go (on foot) | **gaan** | [xān] |
| | | |
| to go for a swim | **gaan zwemmen** | [xān 'zwɛmən] |
| to go out (for dinner, etc.) | **uitgaan** | ['œʏtxān] |
| to guess (the answer) | **goed raden** | [xut 'radən] |
| | | |
| to have (vt) | **hebben** | ['hɛbən] |
| to have breakfast | **ontbijten** | [ɔn'bɛjtən] |
| to have dinner | **souperen** | [su'perən] |
| | | |
| to have lunch | **lunchen** | ['lʉnʃən] |
| to hear (vt) | **horen** | ['hɔrən] |
| | | |
| to help (vt) | **helpen** | ['hɛlpən] |
| to hide (vt) | **verbergen** | [vər'bɛrxən] |
| to hope (vi, vt) | **hopen** | ['hɔpən] |
| to hunt (vi, vt) | **jagen** | ['jaxən] |
| to hurry (vi) | **zich haasten** | [zix 'hāstən] |

## 15. The most important verbs. Part 3

| to inform (vt) | informeren | [infɔr'merən] |
| to insist (vi, vt) | aandringen | ['āndriŋən] |
| to insult (vt) | beledigen | [bə'ledəxən] |
| to invite (vt) | uitnodigen | ['œʏtnɔdixen] |
| to joke (vi) | grappen maken | ['xrapən 'makən] |

| to keep (vt) | bewaren | [bə'warən] |
| to keep silent | zwijgen | ['zwɛjxən] |
| to kill (vt) | doden | ['dɔdən] |
| to know (sb) | kennen | ['kɛnən] |
| to know (sth) | weten | ['wetən] |
| to laugh (vi) | lachen | ['laxən] |

| to liberate (city, etc.) | bevrijden | [bə'vrɛjdən] |
| to like (I like ...) | bevallen | [bə'valən] |
| to look for ... (search) | zoeken | ['zukən] |
| to love (sb) | liefhebben | ['lifhɛbən] |
| to make a mistake | zich vergissen | [zih vər'xisən] |
| to manage, to run | beheren | [bə'herən] |
| to mean (signify) | betekenen | [bə'tekənən] |
| to mention (talk about) | vermelden | [vər'mɛldən] |
| to miss (school, etc.) | verzuimen | [vər'zœʏmən] |
| to notice (see) | opmerken | ['ɔpmɛrkən] |

| to object (vi, vt) | weerspreken | [wēr'sprekən] |
| to observe (see) | waarnemen | ['wārnemən] |
| to open (vt) | openen | ['ɔpənən] |
| to order (meal, etc.) | bestellen | [bə'stɛlən] |
| to order (mil.) | bevelen | [bə'velən] |
| to own (possess) | bezitten | [bə'zitən] |
| to participate (vi) | deelnemen | ['dēlnemən] |
| to pay (vi, vt) | betalen | [bə'talən] |
| to permit (vt) | toestaan | ['tustān] |
| to plan (vt) | plannen | ['planən] |
| to play (children) | spelen | ['spelən] |

| to pray (vi, vt) | bidden | ['bidən] |
| to prefer (vt) | prefereren | [prəfe'rerən] |
| to promise (vt) | beloven | [bə'lɔvən] |
| to pronounce (vt) | uitspreken | ['œʏtsprekən] |
| to propose (vt) | voorstellen | ['vōrstɛlən] |
| to punish (vt) | bestraffen | [bə'strafən] |

## 16. The most important verbs. Part 4

| to read (vi, vt) | lezen | ['lezən] |
| to recommend (vt) | aanbevelen | ['āmbəvelən] |

| | | |
|---|---|---|
| to refuse (vi, vt) | **weigeren** | ['wɛjxərən] |
| to regret (be sorry) | **betreuren** | [bə'trørən] |
| to rent (sth from sb) | **huren** | ['hʉrən] |
| | | |
| to repeat (say again) | **herhalen** | [hɛr'halən] |
| to reserve, to book | **reserveren** | [rezɛr'verən] |
| to run (vi) | **rennen** | ['renən] |
| to save (rescue) | **redden** | ['rɛdən] |
| to say (~ thank you) | **zeggen** | ['zexən] |
| | | |
| to scold (vt) | **uitvaren tegen** | ['œytvarən 'texən] |
| to see (vt) | **zien** | [zin] |
| to sell (vt) | **verkopen** | [vɛr'kɔpən] |
| to send (vt) | **sturen** | ['stʉrən] |
| to shoot (vi) | **schieten** | ['sxitən] |
| | | |
| to shout (vi) | **schreeuwen** | ['sxrēwən] |
| to show (vt) | **tonen** | ['tɔnən] |
| to sign (document) | **ondertekenen** | ['ɔndər'tekənən] |
| to sit down (vi) | **gaan zitten** | [xān 'zitən] |
| | | |
| to smile (vi) | **glimlachen** | ['xlimlahən] |
| to speak (vi, vt) | **spreken** | ['sprekən] |
| to steal (money, etc.) | **stelen** | ['stelən] |
| to stop (for pause, etc.) | **stoppen** | ['stɔpən] |
| to stop (please ~ calling me) | **ophouden** | ['ɔphaudən] |
| | | |
| to study (vt) | **studeren** | [stʉ'derən] |
| to swim (vi) | **zwemmen** | ['zwɛmən] |
| to take (vt) | **nemen** | ['nemən] |
| to think (vi, vt) | **denken** | ['dɛnkən] |
| to threaten (vt) | **bedreigen** | [bə'drɛjxən] |
| | | |
| to touch (with hands) | **aanraken** | ['ānrakən] |
| to translate (vt) | **vertalen** | [vər'talən] |
| to trust (vt) | **vertrouwen** | [vər'trauwən] |
| to try (attempt) | **proberen** | [prɔ'berən] |
| to turn (e.g., ~ left) | **afslaan** | ['afslān] |
| | | |
| to underestimate (vt) | **onderschatten** | ['ɔndər'sxatən] |
| to understand (vt) | **begrijpen** | [bə'xrɛjpən] |
| to unite (vt) | **verenigen** | [və'rɛnixən] |
| to wait (vt) | **wachten** | ['waxtən] |
| | | |
| to want (wish, desire) | **willen** | ['wilən] |
| to warn (vt) | **waarschuwen** | ['wārsxjuvən] |
| to work (vi) | **werken** | ['wɛrkən] |
| to write (vt) | **schrijven** | ['sxrɛjvən] |
| to write down | **opschrijven** | ['ɔpsxrɛjvən] |

BOOKS

T&P

# TIME. CALENDAR

**T&P Books Publishing**

## 17. Weekdays

| | | |
|---|---|---|
| Monday | **maandag (de)** | ['māndax] |
| Tuesday | **dinsdag (de)** | ['dinsdax] |
| Wednesday | **woensdag (de)** | ['wunsdax] |
| Thursday | **donderdag (de)** | ['dɔndərdax] |
| Friday | **vrijdag (de)** | ['vrɛjdax] |
| Saturday | **zaterdag (de)** | ['zatərdax] |
| Sunday | **zondag (de)** | ['zɔndax] |
| | | |
| today (adv) | **vandaag** | [van'dāx] |
| tomorrow (adv) | **morgen** | ['mɔrxən] |
| the day after tomorrow | **overmorgen** | [ɔvər'mɔrxən] |
| yesterday (adv) | **gisteren** | ['xistərən] |
| the day before yesterday | **eergisteren** | [ēr'xistərən] |
| | | |
| day | **dag (de)** | [dax] |
| working day | **werkdag (de)** | ['wɛrk·dax] |
| public holiday | **feestdag (de)** | ['fēst·dax] |
| day off | **verlofdag (de)** | [vər'lɔfdax] |
| weekend | **weekend (het)** | ['wikənt] |
| | | |
| all day long | **de hele dag** | [də 'helə dah] |
| the next day (adv) | **de volgende dag** | [də 'vɔlxəndə dax] |
| two days ago | **twee dagen geleden** | [twē 'daxən xə'ledən] |
| the day before | **aan de vooravond** | [ān də vō'ravɔnt] |
| daily (adj) | **dag-, dagelijks** | [dax], ['daxələks] |
| every day (adv) | **elke dag** | ['ɛlkə dax] |
| | | |
| week | **week (de)** | [wēk] |
| last week (adv) | **vorige week** | ['vɔrixə wēk] |
| next week (adv) | **volgende week** | ['vɔlxəndə wēk] |
| weekly (adj) | **wekelijks** | ['wekələks] |
| every week (adv) | **elke week** | ['ɛlkə wēk] |
| twice a week | **twee keer per week** | [twē ker pər vēk] |
| every Tuesday | **elke dinsdag** | ['ɛlkə 'dinsdax] |

## 18. Hours. Day and night

| | | |
|---|---|---|
| morning | **morgen (de)** | ['mɔrxən] |
| in the morning | **'s morgens** | [s 'mɔrxəns] |
| noon, midday | **middag (de)** | ['midax] |
| in the afternoon | **'s middags** | [s 'midax] |
| evening | **avond (de)** | ['avɔnt] |

| in the evening | 's avonds | [s 'avɔnts] |
| night | nacht (de) | [naxt] |
| at night | 's nachts | [s naxts] |
| midnight | middernacht (de) | ['midər·naxt] |
| | | |
| second | seconde (de) | [se'kɔndə] |
| minute | minuut (de) | [mi'nūt] |
| hour | uur (het) | [ūr] |
| half an hour | halfuur (het) | [half 'ūr] |
| a quarter-hour | kwartier (het) | ['kwar'tir] |
| fifteen minutes | vijftien minuten | ['vɛjftin mi'nʉtən] |
| 24 hours | etmaal (het) | ['ɛtmāl] |
| | | |
| sunrise | zonsopgang (de) | [zɔns'ɔpxaŋ] |
| dawn | dageraad (de) | ['daxərāt] |
| early morning | vroege morgen (de) | ['vruxə 'mɔrxən] |
| sunset | zonsondergang (de) | [zɔns'ɔndərxaŋ] |
| | | |
| early in the morning | 's morgens vroeg | [s 'mɔrxəns vrux] |
| this morning | vanmorgen | [van'mɔrxən] |
| tomorrow morning | morgenochtend | ['mɔrxən·'ɔhtənt] |
| | | |
| this afternoon | vanmiddag | [van'midax] |
| in the afternoon | 's middags | [s 'midax] |
| tomorrow afternoon | morgenmiddag | ['mɔrxən·'midax] |
| | | |
| tonight (this evening) | vanavond | [va'navɔnt] |
| tomorrow night | morgenavond | ['mɔrxən·'avɔnt] |
| | | |
| at 3 o'clock sharp | klokslag drie uur | ['klɔkslax dri ūr] |
| about 4 o'clock | ongeveer vier uur | [ɔnxə'vēr vir ūr] |
| by 12 o'clock | tegen twaalf uur | ['texən twālf ūr] |
| | | |
| in 20 minutes | over twintig minuten | ['ɔvər 'twintix mi'nʉtən] |
| in an hour | over een uur | ['ɔvər en ūr] |
| on time (adv) | op tijd | [ɔp tɛjt] |
| | | |
| a quarter of ... | kwart voor ... | ['kwart võr] |
| within an hour | binnen een uur | ['binən en ūr] |
| every 15 minutes | elk kwartier | ['ɛlk kwar'tir] |
| round the clock | de klok rond | [də klɔk rɔnt] |

## 19. Months. Seasons

| January | januari (de) | [janʉ'ari] |
| February | februari (de) | [febrʉ'ari] |
| March | maart (de) | [mārt] |
| April | april (de) | [ap'ril] |
| May | mei (de) | [mɛj] |
| June | juni (de) | ['juni] |

| | | |
|---|---|---|
| July | juli (de) | ['juli] |
| August | augustus (de) | [au'xʉstʉs] |
| September | september (de) | [sɛp'tɛmbər] |
| October | oktober (de) | [ɔk'tɔbər] |
| November | november (de) | [nɔ'vɛmbər] |
| December | december (de) | [de'sɛmbər] |
| | | |
| spring | lente (de) | ['lɛntə] |
| in spring | in de lente | [in də 'lɛntə] |
| spring (as adj) | lente- | ['lɛntə] |
| | | |
| summer | zomer (de) | ['zɔmər] |
| in summer | in de zomer | [in də 'zɔmər] |
| summer (as adj) | zomer-, zomers | ['zɔmər], ['zɔmərs] |
| | | |
| fall | herfst (de) | [hɛrfst] |
| in fall | in de herfst | [in də hɛrfst] |
| fall (as adj) | herfst- | [hɛrfst] |
| | | |
| winter | winter (de) | ['wintər] |
| in winter | in de winter | [in də 'wintər] |
| winter (as adj) | winter- | ['wintər] |
| | | |
| month | maand (de) | [mānt] |
| this month | deze maand | ['dezə mānt] |
| next month | volgende maand | ['vɔlxəndə mānt] |
| last month | vorige maand | ['vɔrixə mānt] |
| | | |
| a month ago | een maand geleden | [en mānt xə'ledən] |
| in a month (a month later) | over een maand | ['ɔvər en mānt] |
| in 2 months (2 months later) | over twee maanden | ['ɔvər twē 'māndən] |
| the whole month | de hele maand | [də 'helə mānt] |
| all month long | een volle maand | [en 'vɔlə mānt] |
| | | |
| monthly (~ magazine) | maand-, maandelijks | [mānt], ['māndələks] |
| monthly (adv) | maandelijks | ['māndələks] |
| every month | elke maand | ['ɛlkə mānt] |
| twice a month | twee keer per maand | [twē ker per mānt] |
| | | |
| year | jaar (het) | [jār] |
| this year | dit jaar | [dit jār] |
| next year | volgend jaar | ['vɔlxənt jār] |
| last year | vorig jaar | ['vɔrəx jār] |
| | | |
| a year ago | een jaar geleden | [en jār xə'ledən] |
| in a year | over een jaar | ['ɔvər en jār] |
| in two years | over twee jaar | ['ɔvər twē jār] |
| the whole year | het hele jaar | [ət 'helə jār] |
| all year long | een vol jaar | [en vɔl jār] |
| every year | elk jaar | [ɛlk jār] |
| annual (adj) | jaar-, jaarlijks | [jār], ['jārləks] |

| | | |
|---|---|---|
| annually (adv) | **jaarlijks** | ['jārləks] |
| 4 times a year | **4 keer per jaar** | [vir kēr per 'jār] |
| | | |
| date (e.g., today's ~) | **datum (de)** | ['datʉm] |
| date (e.g., ~ of birth) | **datum (de)** | ['datʉm] |
| calendar | **kalender (de)** | [ka'lɛndər] |
| | | |
| half a year | **een half jaar** | [en half jār] |
| six months | **zes maanden** | [zɛs 'māndən] |
| season (summer, etc.) | **seizoen (het)** | [sɛj'zun] |
| century | **eeuw (de)** | [ēw] |

# T&P BOOKS

# TRAVEL. HOTEL

USD  CAD
EUR  CHF
JPY  HKD
GBP  CNY

RECEPTION

**T&P Books Publishing**

| | | |
|---|---|---|
| tourism, travel | toerisme (het) | [tu'rismə] |
| tourist | toerist (de) | [tu'rist] |
| trip, voyage | reis (de) | [rɛjs] |
| adventure | avontuur (het) | [avɔn'tür] |
| trip, journey | tocht (de) | [tɔxt] |
| | | |
| vacation | vakantie (de) | [va'kantsi] |
| to be on vacation | met vakantie zijn | [mɛt va'kantsi zɛjn] |
| rest | rust (de) | [rʉst] |
| | | |
| train | trein (de) | [trɛjn] |
| by train | met de trein | [mɛt də trɛjn] |
| airplane | vliegtuig (het) | ['vlixtœɣx] |
| by airplane | met het vliegtuig | [mɛt ət 'vlixtœɣx] |
| by car | met de auto | [mɛt də 'autɔ] |
| by ship | per schip | [pər sxip] |
| luggage | bagage (de) | [ba'xaʒə] |
| suitcase | valies (de) | [va'lis] |
| luggage cart | bagagekarretje (het) | [ba'xaʒə·'karɛtʃə] |
| | | |
| passport | paspoort (het) | ['paspört] |
| visa | visum (het) | ['vizʉm] |
| ticket | kaartje (het) | ['kärtʃə] |
| air ticket | vliegticket (het) | ['vlix·'tikət] |
| guidebook | reisgids (de) | ['rɛjs·xids] |
| map (tourist ~) | kaart (de) | [kärt] |
| area (rural ~) | gebied (het) | [xə'bit] |
| place, site | plaats (de) | [pläts] |
| | | |
| exotica (n) | exotische bestemming (de) | [ɛ'ksɔtise bɛ'stemiŋ] |
| exotic (adj) | exotisch | [ɛk'sɔtis] |
| amazing (adj) | verwonderlijk | [vər'wɔndərlək] |
| | | |
| group | groep (de) | [xrup] |
| excursion, sightseeing tour | rondleiding (de) | ['rɔntlɛjdiŋ] |
| guide (person) | gids (de) | [xits] |

| | | |
|---|---|---|
| hotel | hotel (het) | [hɔ'tɛl] |
| motel | motel (het) | [mɔ'tɛl] |

| | | |
|---|---|---|
| three-star (~ hotel) | **3-sterren** | [dri-'stɛrən] |
| five-star | **5-sterren** | [vɛjf-'stɛrən] |
| to stay (in a hotel, etc.) | **overnachten** | [ɔvər'naxtən] |
| | | |
| room | **kamer (de)** | ['kamər] |
| single room | **eenpersoonskamer (de)** | [ēnpɛr'sōns·'kamər] |
| double room | **tweepersoonskamer (de)** | [twē·pɛr'sōns·'kamər] |
| to book a room | **een kamer reserveren** | [ən 'kamər rezər'verən] |
| | | |
| half board | **halfpension (het)** | [half·pɛn'ʃɔn] |
| full board | **volpension (het)** | ['vɔl·pɛn'ʃɔn] |
| | | |
| with bath | **met badkamer** | [mɛt 'batkamər] |
| with shower | **met douche** | [mɛt 'duʃ] |
| satellite television | **satelliet-tv (de)** | [satə'lit-te've] |
| air-conditioner | **airconditioner (de)** | [ɛr·kɔn'diʃənər] |
| towel | **handdoek (de)** | ['handuk] |
| key | **sleutel (de)** | ['sløtəl] |
| | | |
| administrator | **administrateur (de)** | [atministra'tør] |
| chambermaid | **kamermeisje (het)** | ['kamər·'mɛjçə] |
| porter, bellboy | **piccolo (de)** | ['pikɔlɔ] |
| doorman | **portier (de)** | [pɔ'rtīr] |
| | | |
| restaurant | **restaurant (het)** | [rɛstɔ'rant] |
| pub, bar | **bar (de)** | [bar] |
| breakfast | **ontbijt (het)** | [ɔn'bɛjt] |
| dinner | **avondeten (het)** | ['avɔntetən] |
| buffet | **buffet (het)** | [bʉ'fɛt] |
| | | |
| lobby | **hal (de)** | [hal] |
| elevator | **lift (de)** | [lift] |
| | | |
| DO NOT DISTURB | **NIET STOREN** | [nit 'stɔrən] |
| NO SMOKING | **VERBODEN TE ROKEN!** | [vər'bɔdən tə 'rɔkən] |

## 22. Sightseeing

| | | |
|---|---|---|
| monument | **monument (het)** | [mɔnʉ'mɛnt] |
| fortress | **vesting (de)** | ['vɛstiŋ] |
| palace | **paleis (het)** | [pa'lɛjs] |
| castle | **kasteel (het)** | [kas'tēl] |
| tower | **toren (de)** | ['tɔrən] |
| mausoleum | **mausoleum (het)** | [mauzɔ'leum] |
| | | |
| architecture | **architectuur (de)** | [arʃitək'tūr] |
| medieval (adj) | **middeleeuws** | ['midəlēws] |
| ancient (adj) | **oud** | ['aut] |
| national (adj) | **nationaal** | [natsjɔ'nāl] |
| famous (monument, etc.) | **bekend** | [bə'kɛnt] |

| | | |
|---|---|---|
| tourist | **toerist (de)** | [tu'rist] |
| guide (person) | **gids (de)** | [xits] |
| excursion, sightseeing tour | **rondleiding (de)** | ['rɔntlɛjdiŋ] |
| to show (vt) | **tonen** | ['tonən] |
| to tell (vt) | **vertellen** | [vər'tɛlən] |
| | | |
| to find (vt) | **vinden** | ['vindən] |
| to get lost (lose one's way) | **verdwalen** | [vərd'walən] |
| map (e.g., subway ~) | **plattegrond (de)** | ['platə·xrɔnt] |
| map (e.g., city ~) | **plattegrond (de)** | ['platə·xrɔnt] |
| | | |
| souvenir, gift | **souvenir (het)** | [suve'nir] |
| gift shop | **souvenirwinkel (de)** | [suve'nir·'winkəl] |
| to take pictures | **foto's maken** | ['fotɔs 'makən] |
| to have one's picture taken | **zich laten fotograferen** | [zih 'latən fotɔxra'ferən] |

# T&P BOOKS

# TRANSPORTATION

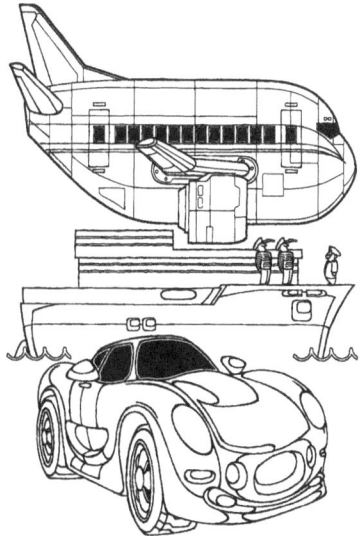

**T&P Books Publishing**

# 23. Airport

| airport | luchthaven (de) | ['lʉxthavən] |
| airplane | vliegtuig (het) | ['vlixtœɣx] |
| airline | luchtvaart- | ['lʉxtvārt |
| | maatschappij (de) | mātsxa'pɛj] |
| air traffic controller | luchtverkeersleider (de) | ['lʉxt·verkērs·'lɛjdər] |

| departure | vertrek (het) | [vər'trɛk] |
| arrival | aankomst (de) | ['ānkɔmst] |
| to arrive (by plane) | aankomen | ['ānkɔmən] |

| departure time | vertrektijd (de) | [vər'trɛk·tɛjt] |
| arrival time | aankomstuur (het) | ['ānkɔmst·'ūr] |

| to be delayed | vertraagd zijn | [vər'trāxt zɛjn] |
| flight delay | vluchtvertraging (de) | ['vlʉxt·vərt'raxiŋ] |

| information board | informatiebord (het) | [infor'matsi·bɔrt] |
| information | informatie (de) | [infor'matsi] |
| to announce (vt) | aankondigen | ['ānkɔndəxən] |
| flight (e.g., next ~) | vlucht (de) | [vlʉxt] |

| customs | douane (de) | [du'anə] |
| customs officer | douanier (de) | [dua'njē] |

| customs declaration | douaneaangifte (de) | [du'anə·'ānxiftə] |
| to fill out (vt) | invullen | ['invʉlən] |
| to fill out the declaration | een douaneaangifte | [en du'anə·'ānxiftə |
| | invullen | 'invʉlən] |
| passport control | paspoortcontrole (de) | ['paspōrt·kɔn'trɔlə] |

| luggage | bagage (de) | [ba'xaʒə] |
| hand luggage | handbagage (de) | [hant·ba'xaʒə] |
| luggage cart | bagagekarretje (het) | [ba'xaʒə·'karɛtʃə] |

| landing | landing (de) | ['landiŋ] |
| landing strip | landingsbaan (de) | ['landiŋs·bān] |
| to land (vi) | landen | ['landən] |
| airstairs | vliegtuigtrap (de) | ['vlixtœɣx·trap] |

| check-in | inchecken (het) | ['intʃɛkən] |
| check-in counter | incheckbalie (de) | ['intʃɛk·'bali] |
| to check-in (vi) | inchecken | ['intʃɛkən] |
| boarding pass | instapkaart (de) | ['instap·kārt] |
| departure gate | gate (de) | [gejt] |

| transit | transit (de) | ['transit] |
| to wait (vt) | wachten | ['waxtən] |
| departure lounge | wachtzaal (de) | ['waxt·zāl] |
| to see off | begeleiden | [bəxə'lɛjdən] |
| to say goodbye | afscheid nemen | ['afsxɛjt 'nemən] |

## 24. Airplane

| airplane | vliegtuig (het) | ['vlixtœɣx] |
| air ticket | vliegticket (het) | ['vlix·'tikət] |
| airline | luchtvaart-maatschappij (de) | ['lʉxtvārt mātsxa'pɛj] |
| airport | luchthaven (de) | ['lʉxthavən] |
| supersonic (adj) | supersonisch | [sʉpər'sɔnis] |

| captain | gezagvoerder (de) | [xəzax·'vurdər] |
| crew | bemanning (de) | [bə'maniŋ] |
| pilot | piloot (de) | [pi'lōt] |
| flight attendant (fem.) | stewardess (de) | [stʉwər'dɛs] |
| navigator | stuurman (de) | ['stūrman] |

| wings | vleugels | ['vløxəls] |
| tail | staart (de) | [stārt] |
| cockpit | cabine (de) | [ka'binə] |
| engine | motor (de) | ['mɔtɔr] |
| undercarriage (landing gear) | landingsgestel (het) | ['landiŋs·xə'stɛl] |
| turbine | turbine (de) | [tʉr'binə] |

| propeller | propeller (de) | [prɔ'pelər] |
| black box | zwarte doos (de) | ['zwartə dōs] |
| yoke (control column) | stuur (het) | [stūr] |
| fuel | brandstof (de) | ['brandstɔf] |

| safety card | veiligheidskaart (de) | ['vɛjləxhɛjts·kārt] |
| oxygen mask | zuurstofmasker (het) | ['zūrstɔf·'maskər] |
| uniform | uniform (het) | ['juniɔrm] |
| life vest | reddingsvest (de) | ['rɛdiŋs·vɛst] |
| parachute | parachute (de) | [para'ʃʉtə] |

| takeoff | opstijgen (het) | ['ɔpstɛjxən] |
| to take off (vi) | opstijgen | ['ɔpstɛjxən] |
| runway | startbaan (de) | ['start·bān] |

| visibility | zicht (het) | [zixt] |
| flight (act of flying) | vlucht (de) | [vlʉxt] |
| altitude | hoogte (de) | ['hōxtə] |
| air pocket | luchtzak (de) | ['lʉxt·zak] |
| seat | plaats (de) | [plāts] |
| headphones | koptelefoon (de) | ['kɔp·telə'fōn] |

| folding tray (tray table) | tafeltje (het) | ['tafɛltʃə] |
| airplane window | venster (het) | ['vɛnstər] |
| aisle | gangpad (het) | ['haŋpat] |

## 25. Train

| train | trein (de) | [trɛjn] |
| commuter train | elektrische trein (de) | [ɛ'lɛktrisə trɛjn] |
| express train | sneltrein (de) | ['snɛl·trɛjn] |
| diesel locomotive | diesellocomotief (de) | ['dizəl·lokomɔ'tif] |
| steam locomotive | stoomlocomotief (de) | [stōm·lokomɔ'tif] |

| passenger car | rijtuig (het) | ['rɛjtœɣx] |
| dining car | restauratierijtuig (het) | [rɛstɔ'ratsi·'rɛjtœɣx] |

| rails | rails | ['rɛjls] |
| railroad | spoorweg (de) | ['spōr·wɛx] |
| railway tie | dwarsligger (de) | ['dwars·lixə] |

| platform (railway ~) | perron (het) | [pɛ'rɔn] |
| track (~ 1, 2, etc.) | spoor (het) | [spōr] |
| semaphore | semafoor (de) | [səma'fōr] |
| station | halte (de) | ['haltə] |

| engineer (train driver) | machinist (de) | [maʃi'nist] |
| porter (of luggage) | kruier (de) | ['krœɣər] |
| car attendant | conducteur (de) | [kɔndʉk'tør] |
| passenger | passagier (de) | [pasa'xir] |
| conductor (ticket inspector) | controleur (de) | [kɔntrɔ'lør] |

| corridor (in train) | gang (de) | [xaŋ] |
| emergency brake | noodrem (de) | ['nōd·rɛm] |

| compartment | coupè (de) | [ku'pɛ] |
| berth | bed (het) | [bɛt] |
| upper berth | bovenste bed (het) | ['bovənstə bɛt] |
| lower berth | onderste bed (het) | ['ɔndərstə bɛt] |
| bed linen, bedding | beddengoed (het) | ['bɛdən·xut] |

| ticket | kaartje (het) | ['kārtʃə] |
| schedule | dienstregeling (de) | [dinst·'rexəliŋ] |
| information display | informatiebord (het) | [infɔr'matsi·bɔrt] |

| to leave, to depart | vertrekken | [vər'trɛkən] |
| departure (of train) | vertrek (het) | [vər'trɛk] |
| to arrive (ab. train) | aankomen | ['ānkomən] |
| arrival | aankomst (de) | ['ānkomst] |
| to arrive by train | aankomen per trein | ['ānkomən pɛr trɛjn] |
| to get on the train | in de trein stappen | [in də 'trɛjn 'stapən] |

| | | |
|---|---|---|
| to get off the train | **uit de trein stappen** | ['œyt də 'trɛjn 'stapən] |
| train wreck | **treinwrak (het)** | ['trɛjn·wrak] |
| to derail (vi) | **ontspoord zijn** | [ɔnt'spŏrt zɛjn] |
| steam locomotive | **stoomlocomotief (de)** | [stŏm·lɔkɔmɔ'tif] |
| stoker, fireman | **stoker (de)** | ['stɔkər] |
| firebox | **stookplaats (de)** | ['stŏk·plãts] |
| coal | **steenkool (de)** | ['stĕn·kŏl] |

## 26. Ship

| | | |
|---|---|---|
| ship | **schip (het)** | [sxip] |
| vessel | **vaartuig (het)** | ['vãrtœyx] |
| | | |
| steamship | **stoomboot (de)** | ['stŏm·bŏt] |
| riverboat | **motorschip (het)** | ['mɔtɔr·sxip] |
| cruise ship | **lijnschip (het)** | ['lɛjn·sxip] |
| cruiser | **kruiser (de)** | ['krœysər] |
| | | |
| yacht | **jacht (het)** | [jaxt] |
| tugboat | **sleepboot (de)** | ['slĕp·bŏt] |
| barge | **duwbak (de)** | ['dʉwbak] |
| ferry | **ferryboot (de)** | ['fɛri·bŏt] |
| | | |
| sailing ship | **zeilboot (de)** | ['zɛjl·bŏt] |
| brigantine | **brigantijn (de)** | [brixan'tɛjn] |
| | | |
| ice breaker | **ijsbreker (de)** | ['ɛjs·brekər] |
| submarine | **duikboot (de)** | ['dœyk·bŏt] |
| | | |
| boat (flat-bottomed ~) | **boot (de)** | [bŏt] |
| dinghy | **sloep (de)** | [slup] |
| lifeboat | **reddingssloep (de)** | ['rɛdiŋs·slup] |
| motorboat | **motorboot (de)** | ['mɔtɔr·bŏt] |
| | | |
| captain | **kapitein (de)** | [kapi'tɛjn] |
| seaman | **zeeman (de)** | ['zĕman] |
| sailor | **matroos (de)** | [ma'trŏs] |
| crew | **bemanning (de)** | [bə'maniŋ] |
| | | |
| boatswain | **bootsman (de)** | ['bŏtsman] |
| ship's boy | **scheepsjongen (de)** | ['sxĕps·'jɔŋən] |
| cook | **kok (de)** | [kɔk] |
| ship's doctor | **scheepsarts (de)** | ['sxĕps·arts] |
| | | |
| deck | **dek (het)** | [dɛk] |
| mast | **mast (de)** | [mast] |
| sail | **zeil (het)** | [zɛjl] |
| | | |
| hold | **ruim (het)** | [rœym] |
| bow (prow) | **voorsteven (de)** | ['vŏrstevən] |

| | | |
|---|---|---|
| stern | achtersteven (de) | ['axtər·stevən] |
| oar | roeispaan (de) | ['rujs·pān] |
| screw propeller | schroef (de) | [sxruf] |
| | | |
| cabin | kajuit (de) | [kajœʏt] |
| wardroom | officierskamer (de) | [ɔfi'sir·'kamər] |
| engine room | machinekamer (de) | [ma'ʃinə·'kamər] |
| bridge | brug (de) | [brʊx] |
| radio room | radiokamer (de) | ['radiɔ·'kamər] |
| wave (radio) | radiogolf (de) | ['radiɔ·xɔlf] |
| logbook | logboek (het) | ['lɔxbuk] |
| | | |
| spyglass | verrekijker (de) | ['vɛrəkɛjkər] |
| bell | klok (de) | [klɔk] |
| flag | vlag (de) | [vlax] |
| | | |
| hawser (mooring ~) | kabel (de) | ['kabəl] |
| knot (bowline, etc.) | knoop (de) | [knōp] |
| | | |
| deckrails | leuning (de) | ['løniŋ] |
| gangway | trap (de) | [trap] |
| | | |
| anchor | anker (het) | ['ankər] |
| to weigh anchor | het anker lichten | [ət 'ankər 'lixtən] |
| to drop anchor | het anker neerlaten | [ət 'ankər 'nērlatən] |
| anchor chain | ankerketting (de) | ['ankər·'ketiŋ] |
| | | |
| port (harbor) | haven (de) | ['havən] |
| quay, wharf | kaai (de) | [kāj] |
| to berth (moor) | aanleggen | ['ānlexən] |
| to cast off | wegvaren | ['wɛxvarən] |
| | | |
| trip, voyage | reis (de) | [rɛjs] |
| cruise (sea trip) | cruise (de) | [krus] |
| course (route) | koers (de) | [kurs] |
| route (itinerary) | route (de) | ['rutə] |
| | | |
| fairway | vaarwater (het) | ['vār·watər] |
| (safe water channel) | | |
| shallows | zandbank (de) | ['zant·bank] |
| to run aground | stranden | ['strandən] |
| | | |
| storm | storm (de) | [stɔrm] |
| signal | signaal (het) | [si'njāl] |
| to sink (vi) | zinken | ['zinkən] |
| Man overboard! | Man overboord! | [man ɔvər'bōrt] |
| SOS (distress signal) | SOS | [ɛs ɔ ɛs] |
| ring buoy | reddingsboei (de) | ['rɛdiŋs·bui] |

# CITY

**T&P Books Publishing**

| | | |
|---|---|---|
| bus | **bus, autobus (de)** | [bʉs], ['autɔbʉs] |
| streetcar | **tram (de)** | [trɛm] |
| trolley bus | **trolleybus (de)** | ['trɔlibʉs] |
| route (of bus, etc.) | **route (de)** | ['rutə] |
| number (e.g., bus ~) | **nummer (het)** | ['nʉmər] |
| | | |
| to go by ... | **rijden met ...** | ['rɛjdən mɛt] |
| to get on (~ the bus) | **stappen** | ['stapən] |
| to get off ... | **afstappen** | ['afstapən] |
| | | |
| stop (e.g., bus ~) | **halte (de)** | ['haltə] |
| next stop | **volgende halte (de)** | ['vɔlxəndə 'haltə] |
| terminus | **eindpunt (het)** | ['ɛjnt·pʉnt] |
| schedule | **dienstregeling (de)** | [dinst·'rexəliŋ] |
| to wait (vt) | **wachten** | ['waxtən] |
| | | |
| ticket | **kaartje (het)** | ['kārtʃə] |
| fare | **reiskosten (de)** | ['rɛjs·kɔstən] |
| | | |
| cashier (ticket seller) | **kassier (de)** | [ka'sir] |
| ticket inspection | **kaartcontrole (de)** | ['kārt·kɔn'trɔlə] |
| ticket inspector | **controleur (de)** | [kɔntrɔ'lør] |
| | | |
| to be late (for ...) | **te laat zijn** | [tə 'lāt zɛjn] |
| to miss (~ the train, etc.) | **missen (de bus ~)** | ['misən] |
| to be in a hurry | **zich haasten** | [zix 'hāstən] |
| | | |
| taxi, cab | **taxi (de)** | ['taksi] |
| taxi driver | **taxichauffeur (de)** | ['taksi·ʃɔ'før] |
| by taxi | **met de taxi** | [mɛt də 'taksi] |
| taxi stand | **taxistandplaats (de)** | ['taksi·'stant·plāts] |
| to call a taxi | **een taxi bestellen** | [en 'taksi bə'stɛlən] |
| to take a taxi | **een taxi nemen** | [en 'taksi 'nemən] |
| | | |
| traffic | **verkeer (het)** | [vər'kēr] |
| traffic jam | **file (de)** | ['filə] |
| rush hour | **spitsuur (het)** | ['spits·ūr] |
| to park (vi) | **parkeren** | [par'kerən] |
| to park (vt) | **parkeren** | [par'kerən] |
| parking lot | **parking (de)** | ['parkiŋ] |
| | | |
| subway | **metro (de)** | ['metrɔ] |
| station | **halte (de)** | ['haltə] |
| to take the subway | **de metro nemen** | [də 'metrɔ 'nemən] |

| train | trein (de) | [trɛjn] |
| train station | station (het) | [sta'tsjɔn] |

## 28. City. Life in the city

| city, town | stad (de) | [stat] |
| capital city | hoofdstad (de) | ['hōft·stat] |
| village | dorp (het) | [dɔrp] |

| city map | plattegrond (de) | ['platə·xrɔnt] |
| downtown | centrum (het) | ['sɛntrʉm] |
| suburb | voorstad (de) | ['vōrstat] |
| suburban (adj) | voorstads- | ['vōrstats] |

| outskirts | randgemeente (de) | ['rant·xəmēntə] |
| environs (suburbs) | omgeving (de) | [ɔm'xeviŋ] |
| city block | blok (het) | [blɔk] |
| residential block (area) | woonwijk (de) | ['wōnvɛjk] |

| traffic | verkeer (het) | [vər'kēr] |
| traffic lights | verkeerslicht (het) | [vər'kērs·lixt] |
| public transportation | openbaar vervoer (het) | [ɔpən'bār vər'vur] |
| intersection | kruispunt (het) | ['krœys·pynt] |

| crosswalk | zebrapad (het) | ['zɛbra·pat] |
| pedestrian underpass | onderdoorgang (de) | ['ɔndər·'dōrxaŋ] |
| to cross (~ the street) | oversteken | [ɔvər'stekən] |
| pedestrian | voetganger (de) | ['vutxaŋər] |
| sidewalk | trottoir (het) | [trɔtu'ar] |

| bridge | brug (de) | [brʉx] |
| embankment (river walk) | dijk (de) | [dɛjk] |
| fountain | fontein (de) | [fɔn'tɛjn] |

| allée (garden walkway) | allee (de) | [a'lē] |
| park | park (het) | [park] |
| boulevard | boulevard (de) | [bulə'var] |
| square | plein (het) | [plɛjn] |
| avenue (wide street) | laan (de) | [lān] |
| street | straat (de) | [strāt] |
| side street | zijstraat (de) | ['zɛj·strāt] |
| dead end | doodlopende straat (de) | [dōd'lɔpəndə strāt] |

| house | huis (het) | ['hœys] |
| building | gebouw (het) | [xə'bau] |
| skyscraper | wolkenkrabber (de) | ['wɔlkən·'krabər] |

| facade | gevel (de) | ['xevəl] |
| roof | dak (het) | [dak] |
| window | venster (het) | ['vɛnstər] |

| arch | boog (de) | [bōx] |
| column | pilaar (de) | [pi'lār] |
| corner | hoek (de) | [huk] |

| store window | vitrine (de) | [vit'rinə] |
| signboard (store sign, etc.) | gevelreclame (de) | ['xevəl·re'klamə] |
| poster | affiche (de/het) | [a'fiʃə] |
| advertising poster | reclameposter (de) | [re'klamə·'pɔstər] |
| billboard | aanplakbord (het) | ['ānplak·'bɔrt] |

| garbage, trash | vuilnis (de/het) | ['vœylnis] |
| trashcan (public ~) | vuilnisbak (de) | ['vœylnis·bak] |
| to litter (vi) | afval weggooien | ['afval 'wɛxōjən] |
| garbage dump | stortplaats (de) | ['stɔrt·plāts] |

| phone booth | telefooncel (de) | [telə'fōn·səl] |
| lamppost | straatlicht (het) | ['strāt·lixt] |
| bench (park ~) | bank (de) | [bank] |

| police officer | politieagent (de) | [pɔ'litsi·a'xɛnt] |
| police | politie (de) | [pɔ'litsi] |
| beggar | zwerver (de) | ['zwɛrvər] |
| homeless (n) | dakloze (de) | [dak'lɔzə] |

## 29. Urban institutions

| store | winkel (de) | ['winkəl] |
| drugstore, pharmacy | apotheek (de) | [apɔ'tēk] |
| eyeglass store | optiek (de) | [ɔp'tik] |
| shopping mall | winkelcentrum (het) | ['winkəl·'sɛntrʉm] |
| supermarket | supermarkt (de) | ['sʉpərmarkt] |

| bakery | bakkerij (de) | ['bakərɛj] |
| baker | bakker (de) | ['bakər] |
| pastry shop | banketbakkerij (de) | [ban'ket·bakə'rɛj] |
| grocery store | kruidenier (de) | [krœydə'nir] |
| butcher shop | slagerij (de) | [slaxə'rɛj] |

| produce store | groentewinkel (de) | ['xruntə·'winkəl] |
| market | markt (de) | [markt] |

| coffee house | koffiehuis (het) | ['kɔfi·hœys] |
| restaurant | restaurant (het) | [rɛstɔ'rant] |
| pub, bar | bar (de) | [bar] |
| pizzeria | pizzeria (de) | [pitsə'rija] |

| hair salon | kapperssalon (de/het) | ['kapərs·sa'lɔn] |
| post office | postkantoor (het) | [pɔst·kan'tōr] |
| dry cleaners | stomerij (de) | [stɔmɛ'rɛj] |
| photo studio | fotostudio (de) | [fotɔ·'stʉdiɔ] |

| shoe store | schoenwinkel (de) | ['sxun·'winkəl] |
| bookstore | boekhandel (de) | ['bukən·'handəl] |
| sporting goods store | sportwinkel (de) | ['spɔrt·'winkəl] |
| | | |
| clothes repair shop | kledingreparatie (de) | ['klediŋ·repa'ratsi] |
| formal wear rental | kledingverhuur (de) | ['klediŋ·vər'hūr] |
| video rental store | videotheek (de) | [videɔ'tēk] |
| | | |
| circus | circus (de/het) | ['sirkʉs] |
| zoo | dierentuin (de) | ['dīrən·tœʏn] |
| movie theater | bioscoop (de) | [biɔ'skōp] |
| museum | museum (het) | [mʉ'zejum] |
| library | bibliotheek (de) | [biblɔ'tēk] |
| | | |
| theater | theater (het) | [te'atər] |
| opera (opera house) | opera (de) | ['ɔpəra] |
| nightclub | nachtclub (de) | ['naxt·klʉp] |
| casino | casino (het) | [ka'sinɔ] |
| | | |
| mosque | moskee (de) | [mɔs'kē] |
| synagogue | synagoge (de) | [sina'xɔxə] |
| cathedral | kathedraal (de) | [kate'drāl] |
| temple | tempel (de) | ['tɛmpəl] |
| church | kerk (de) | [kɛrk] |
| | | |
| college | instituut (het) | [insti'tūt] |
| university | universiteit (de) | [junivɛrsi'tɛjt] |
| school | school (de) | [sxōl] |
| | | |
| prefecture | gemeentehuis (het) | [xə'mēntə·hœʏs] |
| city hall | stadhuis (het) | ['stat·hœʏs] |
| hotel | hotel (het) | [hɔ'tɛl] |
| bank | bank (de) | [bank] |
| | | |
| embassy | ambassade (de) | [amba'sadə] |
| travel agency | reisbureau (het) | [rɛjs·bʉ'rɔ] |
| information office | informatieloket (het) | [infɔr'matsi·lɔ'kɛt] |
| currency exchange | wisselkantoor (het) | ['wisəl·kan'tōr] |
| | | |
| subway | metro (de) | ['metrɔ] |
| hospital | ziekenhuis (het) | ['zikən·hœʏs] |
| | | |
| gas station | benzinestation (het) | [bɛn'zinə·sta'tsjɔn] |
| parking lot | parking (de) | ['parkiŋ] |

## 30. Signs

| signboard (store sign, etc.) | gevelreclame (de) | ['xevəl·re'klamə] |
| notice (door sign, etc.) | opschrift (het) | ['ɔpsxrift] |
| poster | poster (de) | ['pɔstər] |

| direction sign | wegwijzer (de) | ['wɛx·wɛjzər] |
| arrow (sign) | pijl (de) | [pɛjl] |

| caution | waarschuwing (de) | ['wãrsxjuviŋ] |
| warning sign | waarschuwings-<br>bord (het) | ['wãrsxjuviŋs<br>bɔrt] |
| to warn (vt) | waarschuwen | ['wãrsxjuvən] |

| rest day (weekly ~) | vrije dag (de) | ['vrɛjə dax] |
| timetable (schedule) | dienstregeling (de) | [dinst·'rexəliŋ] |
| opening hours | openingsuren | ['ɔpəniŋs·ʉrən] |

| WELCOME! | WELKOM! | ['wɛlkɔm] |
| ENTRANCE | INGANG | ['inxaŋ] |
| EXIT | UITGANG | ['œʏtxaŋ] |
| PUSH | DUWEN | ['dʉwən] |
| PULL | TREKKEN | ['trɛkən] |
| OPEN | OPEN | ['ɔpən] |
| CLOSED | GESLOTEN | [xə'slɔtən] |

| WOMEN | DAMES | ['daməs] |
| MEN | HEREN | ['herən] |

| DISCOUNTS | KORTING | ['kɔrtiŋ] |
| SALE | UITVERKOOP | ['œʏtverkõp] |
| NEW! | NIEUW! | [niu] |
| FREE | GRATIS | ['xratis] |
| ATTENTION! | PAS OP! | [pas 'ɔp] |
| NO VACANCIES | VOLGEBOEKT | ['vɔlxəbukt] |
| RESERVED | GERESERVEERD | [xərezər'vẽrt] |

| ADMINISTRATION | ADMINISTRATIE | [atminist'ratsi] |
| STAFF ONLY | ALLEEN<br>VOOR PERSONEEL | [a'lẽn<br>võr persɔ'nẽl] |

| BEWARE OF THE DOG! | GEVAARLIJKE HOND | [xe'vãrləkə hɔnt] |
| NO SMOKING | VERBODEN TE ROKEN! | [vər'bɔdən tə 'rɔkən] |
| DO NOT TOUCH! | NIET AANRAKEN! | [nit ãn'rakən] |

| DANGEROUS | GEVAARLIJK | [xe'vãrlək] |
| DANGER | GEVAAR | [xe'vãr] |
| HIGH VOLTAGE | HOOGSPANNING | [hõh·'spaniŋ] |
| NO SWIMMING! | VERBODEN<br>TE ZWEMMEN | [vər'bɔdən<br>tə 'zwɛmən] |

| OUT OF ORDER | BUITEN GEBRUIK | ['bœʏtən xəbrœʏk] |
| FLAMMABLE | ONTVLAMBAAR | [ɔnt'flambãr] |
| FORBIDDEN | VERBODEN | [vər'bɔdən] |
| NO TRESPASSING! | DOORGANG VERBODEN | ['dõrxaŋ vər'bɔdən] |
| WET PAINT | OPGELET<br>PAS GEVERFD | [ɔpxe'lɛt<br>pas xə'verft] |

## 31. Shopping

| | | |
|---|---|---|
| to buy (purchase) | **kopen** | ['kɔpən] |
| purchase | **aankoop (de)** | ['ānkɔp] |
| to go shopping | **winkelen** | ['winkelən] |
| shopping | **winkelen (het)** | ['winkelən] |
| | | |
| to be open (ab. store) | **open zijn** | ['ɔpən zɛjn] |
| to be closed | **gesloten zijn** | [xə'slɔtən zɛjn] |
| | | |
| footwear, shoes | **schoeisel (het)** | ['sxuisəl] |
| clothes, clothing | **kleren** (mv.) | ['klerən] |
| cosmetics | **cosmetica** (mv.) | [kɔs'metika] |
| food products | **voedingswaren** | ['vudiŋs·warən] |
| gift, present | **geschenk (het)** | [xə'sxɛnk] |
| | | |
| salesman | **verkoper (de)** | [vər'kɔpər] |
| saleswoman | **verkoopster (de)** | [vər'kõpstər] |
| | | |
| check out, cash desk | **kassa (de)** | ['kasa] |
| mirror | **spiegel (de)** | ['spixəl] |
| counter (store ~) | **toonbank (de)** | ['tõn·bank] |
| fitting room | **paskamer (de)** | ['pas·kamər] |
| | | |
| to try on | **aanpassen** | ['ānpasən] |
| to fit (ab. dress, etc.) | **passen** | ['pasən] |
| to like (I like …) | **bevallen** | [bə'valən] |
| | | |
| price | **prijs (de)** | [prɛjs] |
| price tag | **prijskaartje (het)** | ['prɛjs·'kārtʃə] |
| to cost (vt) | **kosten** | ['kɔstən] |
| How much? | **Hoeveel?** | [hu'vēl] |
| discount | **korting (de)** | ['kɔrtiŋ] |
| | | |
| inexpensive (adj) | **niet duur** | [nit dūr] |
| cheap (adj) | **goedkoop** | [xut'kõp] |
| expensive (adj) | **duur** | [dūr] |
| It's expensive | **Dat is duur.** | [dat is 'dūr] |
| | | |
| rental (n) | **verhuur (de)** | [vər'hūr] |
| to rent (~ a tuxedo) | **huren** | ['hʉrən] |
| credit (trade credit) | **krediet (het)** | [kre'dit] |
| on credit (adv) | **op krediet** | [ɔp kre'dit] |

T&P BOOKS

# CLOTHING & ACCESSORIES

**T&P Books Publishing**

## 32. Outerwear. Coats

| clothes | **kleren** (mv.) | ['klerən] |
| outerwear | **bovenkleding (de)** | ['bɔvən·'klediŋ] |
| winter clothing | **winterkleding (de)** | ['wintər·'klediŋ] |
| | | |
| coat (overcoat) | **jas (de)** | [jas] |
| fur coat | **bontjas (de)** | [bɔnt jas] |
| fur jacket | **bontjasje (het)** | [bɔnt 'jaɕə] |
| down coat | **donzen jas (de)** | ['dɔnzən jas] |
| | | |
| jacket (e.g., leather ~) | **jasje (het)** | ['jaɕə] |
| raincoat (trenchcoat, etc.) | **regenjas (de)** | ['rexən jas] |
| waterproof (adj) | **waterdicht** | ['watərdixt] |

## 33. Men's & women's clothing

| shirt (button shirt) | **overhemd (het)** | ['ɔvərhɛmt] |
| pants | **broek (de)** | [bruk] |
| jeans | **jeans (de)** | [dʒins] |
| suit jacket | **colbert (de)** | ['kɔlbər] |
| suit | **kostuum (het)** | [kɔs'tūm] |
| | | |
| dress (frock) | **jurk (de)** | [jurk] |
| skirt | **rok (de)** | [rɔk] |
| blouse | **blouse (de)** | ['blus] |
| knitted jacket (cardigan, etc.) | **wollen vest (de)** | ['wɔlən vɛst] |
| jacket (of woman's suit) | **blazer (de)** | ['blezər] |
| | | |
| T-shirt | **T-shirt (het)** | ['tiʃøt] |
| shorts (short trousers) | **shorts** | [ʃɔrts] |
| tracksuit | **trainingspak (het)** | ['trɛjniŋs·pak] |
| bathrobe | **badjas (de)** | ['batjas] |
| pajamas | **pyjama (de)** | [pi'jama] |
| | | |
| sweater | **sweater (de)** | ['swetər] |
| pullover | **pullover (de)** | [pʉ'lɔvər] |
| | | |
| vest | **gilet (het)** | [ʒi'lɛt] |
| tailcoat | **rokkostuum (het)** | [rɔk·kɔs'tūm] |
| tuxedo | **smoking (de)** | ['smɔkiŋ] |
| uniform | **uniform (het)** | ['junifɔrm] |
| workwear | **werkkleding (de)** | ['wɛrk·'klediŋ] |

| overalls | overall (de) | [ɔvə'ral] |
| coat (e.g., doctor's smock) | doktersjas (de) | ['dɔktərs jas] |

## 34. Clothing. Underwear

| underwear | ondergoed (het) | ['ɔndərxut] |
| boxers, briefs | herenslip (de) | ['herən·slip] |
| panties | slipjes | ['slipjes] |
| undershirt (A-shirt) | onderhemd (het) | ['ɔndərhɛmt] |
| socks | sokken | ['sɔkən] |
| nightgown | nachthemd (het) | ['naxthɛmt] |
| bra | beha (de) | [be'ha] |
| knee highs (knee-high socks) | kniekousen | [kni·'kausən] |
| pantyhose | panty (de) | ['pɛnti] |
| stockings (thigh highs) | nylonkousen | ['nɛjlon·'kausən] |
| bathing suit | badpak (het) | ['bad·pak] |

## 35. Headwear

| hat | hoed (de) | [hut] |
| fedora | deukhoed (de) | ['døkhut] |
| baseball cap | honkbalpet (de) | ['hɔnkbal·'pɛt] |
| flatcap | kleppet (de) | ['klɛpɛt] |
| beret | baret (de) | [ba'rɛt] |
| hood | kap (de) | [kap] |
| panama hat | panamahoed (de) | [pa'nama·hut] |
| knit cap (knitted hat) | gebreide muts (de) | [xəb'rɛjdə muts] |
| headscarf | hoofddoek (de) | ['hõftduk] |
| women's hat | dameshoed (de) | ['daməs·hut] |
| hard hat | veiligheidshelm (de) | ['vɛjləxhɛjts·hɛlm] |
| garrison cap | veldmuts (de) | ['vɛlt·muts] |
| helmet | helm, valhelm (de) | [hɛlm], ['valhɛlm] |
| derby | bolhoed (de) | ['bɔlhut] |
| top hat | hoge hoed (de) | ['hɔxə hut] |

## 36. Footwear

| footwear | schoeisel (het) | ['sxuisəl] |
| shoes (men's shoes) | schoenen | ['sxunən] |
| shoes (women's shoes) | vrouwenschoenen | ['vrauwən·'sxunən] |

| boots (e.g., cowboy ~) | laarzen | ['lārzən] |
| slippers | pantoffels | [pan'tɔfəls] |

| tennis shoes (e.g., Nike ~) | sportschoenen | ['spɔrt·'sxunən] |
| sneakers | sneakers | ['snikərs] |
| (e.g., Converse ~) | | |
| sandals | sandalen | [san'dalən] |

| cobbler (shoe repairer) | schoenlapper (de) | ['sxun·'lapər] |
| heel | hiel (de) | [hil] |
| pair (of shoes) | paar (het) | [pār] |

| shoestring | veter (de) | ['vetər] |
| to lace (vt) | rijgen | ['rɛjxən] |

| shoehorn | schoenlepel (de) | ['sxun·'lepəl] |
| shoe polish | schoensmeer (de/het) | ['sxun·smēr] |

## 37. Personal accessories

| gloves | handschoenen | ['xand 'sxunən] |
| mittens | wanten | ['wantən] |
| scarf (muffler) | sjaal (de) | [ɕāl] |

| glasses (eyeglasses) | bril (de) | [bril] |
| frame (eyeglass ~) | brilmontuur (het) | [bril·mɔn'tūr] |
| umbrella | paraplu (de) | [parap'lʉ] |
| walking stick | wandelstok (de) | ['wandəl·stɔk] |

| hairbrush | haarborstel (de) | [hār·'bɔrstəl] |
| fan | waaier (de) | ['wājər] |

| tie (necktie) | das (de) | [das] |
| bow tie | strikje (het) | ['strikjə] |

| suspenders | bretels | [brə'tɛls] |
| handkerchief | zakdoek (de) | ['zagduk] |

| comb | kam (de) | [kam] |
| barrette | haarspeldje (het) | [hār·'spɛldjə] |

| hairpin | schuifspeldje (het) | ['sxœɣf·'spɛldjə] |
| buckle | gesp (de) | [xɛsp] |

| belt | broekriem (de) | ['bruk·rim] |
| shoulder strap | draagriem (de) | ['drāx·rim] |

| bag (handbag) | handtas (de) | ['hand·tas] |
| purse | damestas (de) | ['daməs·tas] |
| backpack | rugzak (de) | ['rʉxzak] |

## 38. Clothing. Miscellaneous

| | | |
|---|---|---|
| fashion | mode (de) | ['mɔdə] |
| in vogue (adj) | de mode | [də 'mɔdə] |
| fashion designer | kledingstilist (de) | ['kledɪŋ·sti'list] |
| | | |
| collar | kraag (de) | [krãx] |
| pocket | zak (de) | [zak] |
| pocket (as adj) | zak- | [zak] |
| sleeve | mouw (de) | ['mau] |
| hanging loop | lusje (het) | ['lʉɕə] |
| fly (on trousers) | gulp (de) | [xjulp] |
| | | |
| zipper (fastener) | rits (de) | [rits] |
| fastener | sluiting (de) | ['slœʏtɪŋ] |
| button | knoop (de) | [knõp] |
| buttonhole | knoopsgat (het) | ['knõps·xat] |
| to come off (ab. button) | losraken | [lɔs'rakən] |
| | | |
| to sew (vi, vt) | naaien | ['nãjən] |
| to embroider (vi, vt) | borduren | [bɔr'dʉrən] |
| embroidery | borduursel (het) | [bɔr'dũrsəl] |
| sewing needle | naald (de) | [nãlt] |
| thread | draad (de) | [drãt] |
| seam | naad (de) | [nãt] |
| | | |
| to get dirty (vi) | vies worden | [vis 'wɔrdən] |
| stain (mark, spot) | vlek (de) | [vlɛk] |
| to crease, crumple (vi) | gekreukt raken | [xə'krøkt 'rakən] |
| to tear, to rip (vt) | scheuren | ['sxørən] |
| clothes moth | mot (de) | [mɔt] |

## 39. Personal care. Cosmetics

| | | |
|---|---|---|
| toothpaste | tandpasta (de) | ['tand·pasta] |
| toothbrush | tandenborstel (de) | ['tandən·'bɔrstəl] |
| to brush one's teeth | tanden poetsen | ['tandən 'putsən] |
| | | |
| razor | scheermes (het) | ['sxẽr·mɛs] |
| shaving cream | scheerschuim (het) | [sxẽr·sxœʏm] |
| to shave (vi) | zich scheren | [zix 'sxerən] |
| | | |
| soap | zeep (de) | [zẽp] |
| shampoo | shampoo (de) | ['ʃʌmpõ] |
| | | |
| scissors | schaar (de) | [sxãr] |
| nail file | nagelvijl (de) | ['naxəl·vɛjl] |
| nail clippers | nagelknipper (de) | ['naxəl·'knipər] |
| tweezers | pincet (het) | [pin'sɛt] |

| | | |
|---|---|---|
| cosmetics | cosmetica (mv.) | [kɔs'metika] |
| face mask | masker (het) | ['maskər] |
| manicure | manicure (de) | [mani'kʉrə] |
| to have a manicure | manicure doen | [mani'kʉrə dun] |
| pedicure | pedicure (de) | [pedi'kʉrə] |

| | | |
|---|---|---|
| make-up bag | cosmetica tasje (het) | [kɔs'metika 'taçə] |
| face powder | poeder (de/het) | ['pudər] |
| powder compact | poederdoos (de) | ['pudər·dōs] |
| blusher | rouge (de) | ['ruʒə] |

| | | |
|---|---|---|
| perfume (bottled) | parfum (de/het) | [par'fʉm] |
| toilet water (lotion) | eau de toilet (de) | [ɔ də tua'lɛt] |
| lotion | lotion (de) | [lɔt'ʃɔn] |
| cologne | eau de cologne (de) | [ɔ də kɔ'lɔnjə] |

| | | |
|---|---|---|
| eyeshadow | oogschaduw (de) | ['ōx·sxadʉw] |
| eyeliner | oogpotlood (het) | ['ōx·'pɔtlɔt] |
| mascara | mascara (de) | [mas'kara] |

| | | |
|---|---|---|
| lipstick | lippenstift (de) | ['lipən·stift] |
| nail polish, enamel | nagellak (de) | ['naxəl·lak] |
| hair spray | haarlak (de) | ['hār·lak] |
| deodorant | deodorant (de) | [deɔdɔ'rant] |

| | | |
|---|---|---|
| cream | crème (de) | [krɛ:m] |
| face cream | gezichtscrème (de) | [xə'zihts·krɛ:m] |
| hand cream | handcrème (de) | [hant·krɛ:m] |
| anti-wrinkle cream | antirimpelcrème (de) | [anti'rimpəl·krɛ:m] |
| day cream | dagcrème (de) | ['dax·krɛ:m] |
| night cream | nachtcrème (de) | ['naxt·krɛ:m] |
| day (as adj) | dag- | [dax] |
| night (as adj) | nacht- | [naxt] |

| | | |
|---|---|---|
| tampon | tampon (de) | [tam'pɔn] |
| toilet paper (toilet roll) | toiletpapier (het) | [tua'lɛt·pa'pir] |
| hair dryer | föhn (de) | ['føn] |

## 40. Watches. Clocks

| | | |
|---|---|---|
| watch (wristwatch) | polshorloge (het) | ['pɔls·hɔr'lɔʒə] |
| dial | wijzerplaat (de) | ['wɛjzər·plāt] |
| hand (of clock, watch) | wijzer (de) | ['wɛjzər] |
| metal watch band | metalen horlogeband (de) | [me'talən hɔr'lɔʒə·bant] |
| watch strap | horlogebandje (het) | [hɔr'lɔʒə·'bandjə] |

| | | |
|---|---|---|
| battery | batterij (de) | [batə'rɛj] |
| to be dead (battery) | leeg zijn | [lēx zɛjn] |
| to change a battery | batterij vervangen | [batə'rɛj vər'vaŋən] |

| to run fast | **voorlopen** | ['vōrlɔpən] |
| to run slow | **achterlopen** | ['axtərlɔpən] |
| | | |
| wall clock | **wandklok (de)** | ['want·klɔk] |
| hourglass | **zandloper (de)** | ['zant·lopər] |
| sundial | **zonnewijzer (de)** | ['zɔnə·wɛjzər] |
| alarm clock | **wekker (de)** | ['wɛkər] |
| watchmaker | **horlogemaker (de)** | [hɔr'lɔʒə·'makər] |
| to repair (vt) | **repareren** | [repa'rerən] |

T&P BOOKS

# EVERYDAY EXPERIENCE

T&P Books Publishing

| | | |
|---|---|---|
| money | geld (het) | [xɛlt] |
| currency exchange | ruil (de) | [rœyl] |
| exchange rate | koers (de) | [kurs] |
| ATM | geldautomaat (de) | [xɛlt·autoˈmāt] |
| coin | muntstuk (de) | [ˈmʉntstʉk] |
| | | |
| dollar | dollar (de) | [ˈdɔlar] |
| euro | euro (de) | [ørɔ] |
| | | |
| lira | lire (de) | [ˈlirə] |
| Deutschmark | Duitse mark (de) | [ˈdœʏtsə mark] |
| franc | frank (de) | [frank] |
| pound sterling | pond sterling (het) | [pɔnt ˈstɛrliŋ] |
| yen | yen (de) | [jen] |
| | | |
| debt | schuld (de) | [sxʉlt] |
| debtor | schuldenaar (de) | [ˈsxʉldənār] |
| to lend (money) | uitlenen | [ˈœʏtlənən] |
| to borrow (vi, vt) | lenen | [ˈlenən] |
| | | |
| bank | bank (de) | [bank] |
| account | bankrekening (de) | [bank·ˈrekəniŋ] |
| to deposit (vt) | storten | [ˈstɔrtən] |
| to deposit into the account | op rekening storten | [ɔp ˈrekəniŋ ˈstɔrtən] |
| to withdraw (vt) | opnemen | [ˈɔpnemən] |
| | | |
| credit card | kredietkaart (de) | [kreˈdit·kārt] |
| cash | baar geld (het) | [bār ˈxɛlt] |
| check | cheque (de) | [ʃɛk] |
| to write a check | een cheque uitschrijven | [en ʃɛk œʏtˈsxrɛjvən] |
| checkbook | chequeboekje (het) | [ʃɛk·ˈbukjə] |
| | | |
| wallet | portefeuille (de) | [pɔrtəˈfœʏə] |
| change purse | geldbeugel (de) | [xɛlt·ˈbøxəl] |
| safe | safe (de) | [sef] |
| | | |
| heir | erfgenaam (de) | [ˈɛrfxənām] |
| inheritance | erfenis (de) | [ˈɛrfənis] |
| fortune (wealth) | fortuin (het) | [fɔrˈtœʏn] |
| | | |
| lease | huur (de) | [hūr] |
| rent (money) | huurprijs (de) | [ˈhūr·prɛjs] |
| to rent (sth from sb) | huren | [ˈhʉrən] |
| price | prijs (de) | [prɛjs] |

| cost | kostprijs (de) | ['kɔstprɛjs] |
| sum | som (de) | [sɔm] |

| to spend (vt) | uitgeven | ['œʏtxevən] |
| expenses | kosten | ['kɔstən] |
| to economize (vi, vt) | bezuinigen | [bə'zœʏnəxən] |
| economical | zuinig | ['zœʏnəx] |

| to pay (vi, vt) | betalen | [bə'talən] |
| payment | betaling (de) | [bə'taliŋ] |
| change (give the ~) | wisselgeld (het) | ['wisəl·xɛlt] |

| tax | belasting (de) | [bə'lastiŋ] |
| fine | boete (de) | ['butə] |
| to fine (vt) | beboeten | [bə'butən] |

## 42. Post. Postal service

| post office | postkantoor (het) | [pɔst·kan'tōr] |
| mail (letters, etc.) | post (de) | [pɔst] |
| mailman | postbode (de) | ['pɔst·bodə] |
| opening hours | openingsuren | ['ɔpəniŋs·ʉrən] |

| letter | brief (de) | [brif] |
| registered letter | aangetekende brief (de) | ['ānxə'tekəndə brif] |
| postcard | briefkaart (de) | ['brif·kārt] |
| telegram | telegram (het) | [teləx'ram] |
| package (parcel) | postpakket (het) | [pɔstpa'ket] |
| money transfer | overschrijving (de) | [ɔvər'sxrɛjviŋ] |

| to receive (vt) | ontvangen | [ɔnt'faŋən] |
| to send (vt) | sturen | ['stʉrən] |
| sending | verzending (de) | [vər'zɛndiŋ] |

| address | adres (het) | [ad'rɛs] |
| ZIP code | postcode (de) | ['pɔst·kodə] |
| sender | verzender (de) | [vər'zɛndər] |
| receiver | ontvanger (de) | [ɔnt'faŋər] |

| name (first name) | naam (de) | [nām] |
| surname (last name) | achternaam (de) | ['axtər·nām] |

| postage rate | tarief (het) | [ta'rif] |
| standard (adj) | standaard | ['standārt] |
| economical (adj) | zuinig | ['zœʏnəx] |

| weight | gewicht (het) | [xə'wixt] |
| to weigh (~ letters) | afwegen | ['afwexən] |
| envelope | envelop (de) | [ɛnve'lɔp] |
| postage stamp | postzegel (de) | ['pɔst·zexəl] |

| to stamp an envelope | een postzegel plakken op | [en pɔst'zexəl 'plakən ɔp] |

## 43. Banking

| bank | bank (de) | [bank] |
| branch (of bank, etc.) | bankfiliaal (het) | [bank·fili'āl] |

| bank clerk, consultant | bankbediende (de) | [bank·bə'dində] |
| manager (director) | manager (de) | ['mɛnədʒər] |

| bank account | bankrekening (de) | [bank·'rekəniŋ] |
| account number | rekeningnummer (het) | ['rekəniŋ·'nʉmər] |
| checking account | lopende rekening (de) | ['lɔpəndə 'rekəniŋ] |
| savings account | spaarrekening (de) | ['spār·'rekəniŋ] |

| to open an account | een rekening openen | [en 'rekəniŋ 'ɔpənən] |
| to close the account | de rekening sluiten | [də 'rekəniŋ slœytən] |
| to deposit into the account | op rekening storten | [ɔp 'rekəniŋ 'stɔrtən] |
| to withdraw (vt) | opnemen | ['ɔpnemən] |

| deposit | storting (de) | ['stɔrtiŋ] |
| to make a deposit | een storting maken | [en 'stɔrtiŋ 'makən] |

| wire transfer | overschrijving (de) | [ɔvər'sxrɛjviŋ] |
| to wire, to transfer | een overschrijving maken | [en ɔvər'sxrɛjviŋ 'makən] |

| sum | som (de) | [sɔm] |
| How much? | Hoeveel? | [hu'vēl] |

| signature | handtekening (de) | ['hand·'tekəniŋ] |
| to sign (vt) | ondertekenen | ['ɔndər'tekənən] |

| credit card | kredietkaart (de) | [kre'dit·kārt] |
| code (PIN code) | code (de) | ['kɔdə] |

| credit card number | kredietkaart-nummer (het) | [kre'dit·kārt 'nʉmər] |
| ATM | geldautomaat (de) | [xɛlt·auto'māt] |

| check | cheque (de) | [ʃɛk] |
| to write a check | een cheque uitschrijven | [en ʃɛk œyt'sxrɛjvən] |
| checkbook | chequeboekje (het) | [ʃɛk·'bukjə] |

| loan (bank ~) | lening, krediet (de) | ['leniŋ], [kre'dit] |
| to apply for a loan | een lening aanvragen | [en 'leniŋ 'ānvraxən] |
| to get a loan | een lening nemen | [en 'leniŋ 'nemən] |
| to give a loan | een lening verlenen | [en 'leniŋ vər'lenən] |
| guarantee | garantie (de) | [xa'rantsi] |

## 44. Telephone. Phone conversation

| telephone | telefoon (de) | [teleˈfõn] |
| cell phone | mobieltje (het) | [mɔˈbiltʃe] |
| answering machine | antwoordapparaat (het) | [ˈantwõrt·apaˈrāt] |
| | | |
| to call (by phone) | bellen | [ˈbelen] |
| phone call | belletje (het) | [ˈbeletʃe] |
| | | |
| to dial a number | een nummer draaien | [en ˈnʉmer ˈdrājen] |
| Hello! | Hallo! | [haˈlɔ] |
| to ask (vt) | vragen | [ˈvraxen] |
| to answer (vi, vt) | antwoorden | [ˈantwõrden] |
| | | |
| to hear (vt) | horen | [ˈhɔren] |
| well (adv) | goed | [xut] |
| not well (adv) | slecht | [slɛxt] |
| noises (interference) | storingen | [ˈstɔriŋen] |
| | | |
| receiver | hoorn (de) | [hõrn] |
| to pick up (~ the phone) | opnemen | [ˈɔpnemen] |
| to hang up (~ the phone) | ophangen | [ˈɔphaŋen] |
| | | |
| busy (engaged) | bezet | [beˈzɛt] |
| to ring (ab. phone) | overgaan | [ˈɔverxān] |
| telephone book | telefoonboek (het) | [teleˈfõn·buk] |
| | | |
| local (adj) | lokaal | [lɔˈkāl] |
| local call | lokaal gesprek (het) | [lɔˈkāl xespˈrɛk] |
| long distance (~ call) | interlokaal | [interlɔˈkāl] |
| long-distance call | interlokaal gesprek (het) | [interlɔˈkāl xeˈsprɛk] |
| international (adj) | buitenlands | [ˈbœʏtenlants] |
| international call | buitenlands gesprek (het) | [ˈbœʏtenlants xeˈʃprɛk] |

## 45. Cell phone

| cell phone | mobieltje (het) | [mɔˈbiltʃe] |
| display | scherm (het) | [sxɛrm] |
| button | toets, knop (de) | [tuts], [knɔp] |
| SIM card | simkaart (de) | [ˈsim·kārt] |
| | | |
| battery | batterij (de) | [bateˈrɛj] |
| to be dead (battery) | leeg zijn | [lēx zɛjn] |
| charger | acculader (de) | [akʉˈlader] |
| | | |
| menu | menu (het) | [meˈnʉ] |
| settings | instellingen | [ˈinstɛliŋen] |
| tune (melody) | melodie (de) | [melɔˈdi] |

| | | |
|---|---|---|
| to select (vt) | selecteren | [sɛlɛk'terən] |
| calculator | rekenmachine (de) | ['rekən·ma'ʃinə] |
| voice mail | voicemail (de) | ['vɔjs·mɛjl] |
| alarm clock | wekker (de) | ['wɛkər] |
| contacts | contacten | [kɔn'taktən] |
| | | |
| SMS (text message) | SMS-bericht (het) | [ɛsɛ'mɛs-bə'rixt] |
| subscriber | abonnee (de) | [abɔ'ně] |

## 46. Stationery

| | | |
|---|---|---|
| ballpoint pen | balpen (de) | ['bal·pən] |
| fountain pen | vulpen (de) | ['vʉl·pən] |
| | | |
| pencil | potlood (het) | ['pɔtlōt] |
| highlighter | marker (de) | ['markər] |
| felt-tip pen | viltstift (de) | ['vilt·stift] |
| | | |
| notepad | notitieboekje (het) | [nɔ'titsi·'bukje] |
| agenda (diary) | agenda (de) | [a'xɛnda] |
| | | |
| ruler | liniaal (de/het) | [lini'āl] |
| calculator | rekenmachine (de) | ['rekən·ma'ʃinə] |
| eraser | gom (de) | [xɔm] |
| thumbtack | punaise (de) | [pʉ'nɛzə] |
| paper clip | paperclip (de) | ['pɛjpər·klip] |
| | | |
| glue | lijm (de) | [lɛjm] |
| stapler | nietmachine (de) | ['nit·ma'ʃinə] |
| hole punch | perforator (de) | [pɛrfɔ'ratɔr] |
| pencil sharpener | potloodslijper (de) | ['pɔtlōt·'slɛjpər] |

## 47. Foreign languages

| | | |
|---|---|---|
| language | taal (de) | [tāl] |
| foreign (adj) | vreemd | [vrēmt] |
| foreign language | vreemde taal (de) | ['vrēmdə tāl] |
| to study (vt) | leren | ['lerən] |
| to learn (language, etc.) | studeren | [stʉ'derən] |
| | | |
| to read (vi, vt) | lezen | ['lezən] |
| to speak (vi, vt) | spreken | ['sprekən] |
| to understand (vt) | begrijpen | [bə'xrɛjpən] |
| to write (vt) | schrijven | ['sxrɛjvən] |
| | | |
| fast (adv) | snel | [snɛl] |
| slowly (adv) | langzaam | ['laŋzām] |
| fluently (adv) | vloeiend | ['vlujənt] |

| rules | regels | ['rexəls] |
|---|---|---|
| grammar | grammatica (de) | [xra'matika] |
| vocabulary | vocabulaire (het) | [vɔkabʉ'lɛːr] |
| phonetics | fonetiek (de) | [fɔnɛ'tik] |

| textbook | leerboek (het) | ['lēr·buk] |
|---|---|---|
| dictionary | woordenboek (het) | ['wōrdən·buk] |
| teach-yourself book | leerboek (het) voor zelfstudie | ['lērbuk vōr 'zɛlfstʉdi] |
| phrasebook | taalgids (de) | ['tāl·xits] |

| cassette, tape | cassette (de) | [ka'sɛtə] |
|---|---|---|
| videotape | videocassette (de) | ['video·ka'sɛtə] |
| CD, compact disc | CD (de) | [se'de] |
| DVD | DVD (de) | [deve'de] |

| alphabet | alfabet (het) | ['alfabət] |
|---|---|---|
| to spell (vt) | spellen | ['spɛlən] |
| pronunciation | uitspraak (de) | ['œʏtsprāk] |

| accent | accent (het) | [ak'sɛnt] |
|---|---|---|
| with an accent | met een accent | [mɛt en ak'sɛnt] |
| without an accent | zonder accent | ['zɔndər ak'sɛnt] |

| word | woord (het) | [wōrt] |
|---|---|---|
| meaning | betekenis (de) | [bə'tekənis] |

| course (e.g., a French ~) | cursus (de) | ['kʉrzʉs] |
|---|---|---|
| to sign up | zich inschrijven | [zix 'insxrɛjvən] |
| teacher | leraar (de) | ['lerār] |

| translation (process) | vertaling (de) | [vər'taliŋ] |
|---|---|---|
| translation (text, etc.) | vertaling (de) | [vər'taliŋ] |
| translator | vertaler (de) | [vər'talər] |
| interpreter | tolk (de) | [tɔlk] |

| polyglot | polyglot (de) | [poli'xlɔt] |
|---|---|---|
| memory | geheugen (het) | [xə'høxən] |

T&P BOOKS

# MEALS. RESTAURANT

T&P Books Publishing

## 48. Table setting

| | | |
|---|---|---|
| spoon | lepel (de) | ['lepəl] |
| knife | mes (het) | [mɛs] |
| fork | vork (de) | [vɔrk] |
| | | |
| cup (e.g., coffee ~) | kopje (het) | ['kɔpjə] |
| plate (dinner ~) | bord (het) | [bɔrt] |
| saucer | schoteltje (het) | ['sxɔteltʃə] |
| napkin (on table) | servet (het) | [sɛr'vɛt] |
| toothpick | tandenstoker (de) | ['tandən·'stɔkər] |

## 49. Restaurant

| | | |
|---|---|---|
| restaurant | restaurant (het) | [rɛstɔ'rant] |
| coffee house | koffiehuis (het) | ['kɔfi·hœys] |
| pub, bar | bar (de) | [bar] |
| tearoom | tearoom (de) | ['ti·rōm] |
| | | |
| waiter | kelner, ober (de) | ['kɛlnər], ['ɔbər] |
| waitress | serveerster (de) | [sɛr'vērstər] |
| bartender | barman (de) | ['barman] |
| menu | menu (het) | [me'nʉ] |
| wine list | wijnkaart (de) | ['wɛjn·kārt] |
| to book a table | een tafel reserveren | [en 'tafəl rezər'verən] |
| course, dish | gerecht (het) | [xe'rɛht] |
| to order (meal) | bestellen | [bə'stɛlən] |
| to make an order | een bestelling maken | [en bə'stɛliŋ 'makən] |
| | | |
| aperitif | aperitief (de/het) | [aperi'tif] |
| appetizer | voorgerecht (het) | ['vōrxərɛht] |
| dessert | dessert (het) | [dɛ'sɛːr] |
| | | |
| check | rekening (de) | ['rekəniŋ] |
| to pay the check | de rekening betalen | [də 'rekəniŋ bə'talən] |
| to give change | wisselgeld teruggeven | ['wisəl·xɛlt tɛ'rʉxevən] |
| tip | fooi (de) | [fōj] |

## 50. Meals

| | | |
|---|---|---|
| food | eten (het) | ['etən] |
| to eat (vi, vt) | eten | ['etən] |

| | | |
|---|---|---|
| breakfast | **ontbijt (het)** | [ɔn'bɛjt] |
| to have breakfast | **ontbijten** | [ɔn'bɛjtən] |
| lunch | **lunch (de)** | ['lʉnʃ] |
| to have lunch | **lunchen** | ['lʉnʃən] |
| dinner | **avondeten (het)** | ['avɔntetən] |
| to have dinner | **souperen** | [su'perən] |
| | | |
| appetite | **eetlust (de)** | ['ētlʉst] |
| Enjoy your meal! | **Eet smakelijk!** | [ēt 'smakələk] |
| | | |
| to open (~ a bottle) | **openen** | ['ɔpənən] |
| to spill (liquid) | **morsen** | ['mɔrsən] |
| to spill out (vi) | **zijn gemorst** | [zɛjn xɛ'mɔrst] |
| | | |
| to boil (vi) | **koken** | ['kɔkən] |
| to boil (vt) | **koken** | ['kɔkən] |
| boiled (~ water) | **gekookt** | [xə'kōkt] |
| to chill, cool down (vt) | **afkoelen** | ['afkulən] |
| to chill (vi) | **afkoelen** | ['afkulən] |
| | | |
| taste, flavor | **smaak (de)** | [smāk] |
| aftertaste | **nasmaak (de)** | ['nasmāk] |
| | | |
| to slim down (lose weight) | **volgen een dieet** | ['vɔlxə en di'ēt] |
| diet | **dieet (het)** | [di'ēt] |
| vitamin | **vitamine (de)** | [vita'minə] |
| calorie | **calorie (de)** | [kalɔ'ri] |
| vegetarian (n) | **vegetariër (de)** | [vəxɛ'tarier] |
| vegetarian (adj) | **vegetarisch** | [vəxɛ'taris] |
| | | |
| fats (nutrient) | **vetten** | ['vɛtən] |
| proteins | **eiwitten** | ['ɛjwitən] |
| carbohydrates | **koolhydraten** | [kōlhi'dratən] |
| slice (of lemon, ham) | **snede (de)** | ['snedə] |
| piece (of cake, pie) | **stuk (het)** | [stʉk] |
| crumb (of bread, cake, etc.) | **kruimel (de)** | ['krœʏməl] |

## 51. Cooked dishes

| | | |
|---|---|---|
| course, dish | **gerecht (het)** | [xe'rɛht] |
| cuisine | **keuken (de)** | ['køkən] |
| recipe | **recept (het)** | [re'sɛpt] |
| portion | **portie (de)** | ['pɔrsi] |
| | | |
| salad | **salade (de)** | [sa'ladə] |
| soup | **soep (de)** | [sup] |
| | | |
| clear soup (broth) | **bouillon (de)** | [bu'jon] |
| sandwich (bread) | **boterham (de)** | ['bɔtərham] |

| fried eggs | spiegelei (het) | ['spixəl·ɛj] |
| hamburger (beefburger) | hamburger (de) | ['hambʉrxər] |
| beefsteak | biefstuk (de) | ['bifstʉk] |

| side dish | garnering (de) | [xar'neriŋ] |
| spaghetti | spaghetti (de) | [spa'xeti] |
| mashed potatoes | aardappelpuree (de) | ['ārdapəl·pʉ'rē] |
| pizza | pizza (de) | ['pitsa] |
| porridge (oatmeal, etc.) | pap (de) | [pap] |
| omelet | omelet (de) | [ɔmə'lɛt] |

| boiled (e.g., ~ beef) | gekookt | [xə'kōkt] |
| smoked (adj) | gerookt | [xə'rōkt] |
| fried (adj) | gebakken | [xə'bakən] |
| dried (adj) | gedroogd | [xə'drōxt] |
| frozen (adj) | diepvries | ['dip·vris] |
| pickled (adj) | gemarineerd | [xəmari'nērt] |

| sweet (sugary) | zoet | [zut] |
| salty (adj) | gezouten | [xə'zautən] |
| cold (adj) | koud | ['kaut] |
| hot (adj) | heet | [hēt] |
| bitter (adj) | bitter | ['bitər] |
| tasty (adj) | lekker | ['lɛkər] |

| to cook in boiling water | koken | ['kɔkən] |
| to cook (dinner) | bereiden | [bə'rɛjdən] |
| to fry (vt) | bakken | ['bakən] |
| to heat up (food) | opwarmen | ['ɔpwarmən] |

| to salt (vt) | zouten | ['zautən] |
| to pepper (vt) | peperen | ['pepərən] |
| to grate (vt) | raspen | ['raspən] |
| peel (n) | schil (de) | [sxil] |
| to peel (vt) | schillen | ['sxilən] |

## 52. Food

| meat | vlees (het) | [vlēs] |
| chicken | kip (de) | [kip] |
| Rock Cornish hen (poussin) | kuiken (het) | ['kœʏkən] |
| duck | eend (de) | [ēnt] |
| goose | gans (de) | [xans] |
| game | wild (het) | [wilt] |
| turkey | kalkoen (de) | [kal'kun] |

| pork | varkensvlees (het) | ['varkəns·vlēs] |
| veal | kalfsvlees (het) | ['kalfs·vlēs] |
| lamb | schapenvlees (het) | ['sxapən·vlēs] |

| | | |
|---|---|---|
| beef | **rundvlees (het)** | ['runt·vlēs] |
| rabbit | **konijnenvlees (het)** | [kɔ'nɛjnən·vlēs] |
| sausage (bologna, pepperoni, etc.) | **worst (de)** | [wɔrst] |
| vienna sausage (frankfurter) | **saucijs (de)** | ['sɔsɛjs] |
| bacon | **spek (het)** | [spɛk] |
| ham | **ham (de)** | [ham] |
| gammon | **gerookte achterham (de)** | [xə'rōktə 'ahtərham] |
| pâté | **paté (de)** | [pa'tɛ] |
| liver | **lever (de)** | ['levər] |
| hamburger (ground beef) | **gehakt (het)** | [xə'hakt] |
| tongue | **tong (de)** | [tɔŋ] |
| egg | **ei (het)** | [ɛj] |
| eggs | **eieren** | ['ɛjerən] |
| egg white | **eiwit (het)** | ['ɛjwit] |
| egg yolk | **eigeel (het)** | ['ɛjxēl] |
| fish | **vis (de)** | [vis] |
| seafood | **zeevruchten** | [zē·'vrʉxtən] |
| crustaceans | **schaaldieren** | ['sxal·dīrən] |
| caviar | **kaviaar (de)** | [ka'vjãr] |
| crab | **krab (de)** | [krab] |
| shrimp | **garnaal (de)** | [xar'nãl] |
| oyster | **oester (de)** | ['ustər] |
| spiny lobster | **langoest (de)** | [lan'xust] |
| octopus | **octopus (de)** | ['ɔktɔpʉs] |
| squid | **inktvis (de)** | ['inktvis] |
| sturgeon | **steur (de)** | ['stør] |
| salmon | **zalm (de)** | [zalm] |
| halibut | **heilbot (de)** | ['hɛjlbɔt] |
| cod | **kabeljauw (de)** | [kabə'ljau] |
| mackerel | **makreel (de)** | [ma'krēl] |
| tuna | **tonijn (de)** | [tɔ'nɛjn] |
| eel | **paling (de)** | [pa'liŋ] |
| trout | **forel (de)** | [fɔ'rɛl] |
| sardine | **sardine (de)** | [sar'dinə] |
| pike | **snoek (de)** | [snuk] |
| herring | **haring (de)** | ['hariŋ] |
| bread | **brood (het)** | [brōt] |
| cheese | **kaas (de)** | [kãs] |
| sugar | **suiker (de)** | [sœɣkər] |
| salt | **zout (het)** | ['zaut] |
| rice | **rijst (de)** | [rɛjst] |

| pasta (macaroni) | pasta (de) | ['pasta] |
| noodles | noedels | ['nudɛls] |

| butter | boter (de) | ['botər] |
| vegetable oil | plantaardige olie (de) | [plant'ārdixə 'ɔli] |
| sunflower oil | zonnebloemolie (de) | ['zɔnəblum·'ɔli] |
| margarine | margarine (de) | [marxa'rinə] |

| olives | olijven | [ɔ'lɛjvən] |
| olive oil | olijfolie (de) | [ɔ'lɛjf·'ɔli] |

| milk | melk (de) | [mɛlk] |
| condensed milk | gecondenseerde melk (de) | [xəkɔnsən'sērdə mɛlk] |
| yogurt | yoghurt (de) | ['jogʉrt] |
| sour cream | zure room (de) | ['zʉrə rōm] |
| cream (of milk) | room (de) | [rōm] |

| mayonnaise | mayonaise (de) | [majo'nɛzə] |
| buttercream | crème (de) | [krɛːm] |

| cereal grains (wheat, etc.) | graan (het) | [xrān] |
| flour | meel (het), bloem (de) | [mēl], [blum] |
| canned food | conserven | [kɔn'sɛrvən] |

| cornflakes | maïsvlokken | [majs·'vlɔkən] |
| honey | honing (de) | ['hɔniŋ] |
| jam | jam (de) | [ʃɛm] |
| chewing gum | kauwgom (de) | ['kauxɔm] |

## 53. Drinks

| water | water (het) | ['watər] |
| drinking water | drinkwater (het) | ['drink·'watər] |
| mineral water | mineraalwater (het) | [minə'rāl·'watər] |

| still (adj) | zonder gas | ['zɔndər xas] |
| carbonated (adj) | koolzuurhoudend | [kōlzūr·'haudənt] |
| sparkling (adj) | bruisend | ['brœʏsənt] |
| ice | ijs (het) | [ɛjs] |
| with ice | met ijs | [mɛt ɛjs] |

| non-alcoholic (adj) | alcohol vrij | ['alkɔhɔl vrɛj] |
| soft drink | alcohol vrije drank (de) | ['alkɔhɔl 'vrɛjə drank] |
| refreshing drink | frisdrank (de) | ['fris·drank] |
| lemonade | limonade (de) | [limɔ'nadə] |

| liquors | alcoholische dranken | [alkɔ'holisə 'drankən] |
| wine | wijn (de) | [wɛjn] |

| | | |
|---|---|---|
| white wine | **witte wijn (de)** | ['witə wɛjn] |
| red wine | **rode wijn (de)** | ['rɔdə wɛjn] |
| | | |
| liqueur | **likeur (de)** | [li'kør] |
| champagne | **champagne (de)** | [ʃʌm'panjə] |
| vermouth | **vermout (de)** | ['vɛrmut] |
| | | |
| whiskey | **whisky (de)** | ['wiski] |
| vodka | **wodka (de)** | ['wɔdka] |
| gin | **gin (de)** | [dʒin] |
| cognac | **cognac (de)** | [kɔ'njak] |
| rum | **rum (de)** | [rʉm] |
| | | |
| coffee | **koffie (de)** | ['kɔfi] |
| black coffee | **zwarte koffie (de)** | ['zwartə 'kɔfi] |
| coffee with milk | **koffie (de) met melk** | ['kɔfi mɛt mɛlk] |
| cappuccino | **cappuccino (de)** | [kapu'tʃinɔ] |
| instant coffee | **oploskoffie (de)** | ['ɔplɔs·'kɔfi] |
| | | |
| milk | **melk (de)** | [mɛlk] |
| cocktail | **cocktail (de)** | ['kɔktəl] |
| milkshake | **milkshake (de)** | ['milk·ʃɛjk] |
| | | |
| juice | **sap (het)** | [sap] |
| tomato juice | **tomatensap (het)** | [tɔ'matən·sap] |
| orange juice | **sinaasappelsap (het)** | ['sināsapəl·sap] |
| freshly squeezed juice | **vers geperst sap (het)** | [vɛrs xə'pɛrst sap] |
| | | |
| beer | **bier (het)** | [bir] |
| light beer | **licht bier (het)** | [lixt bir] |
| dark beer | **donker bier (het)** | ['dɔnkər bir] |
| | | |
| tea | **thee (de)** | [tē] |
| black tea | **zwarte thee (de)** | ['zwartə tē] |
| green tea | **groene thee (de)** | ['xrunə tē] |

## 54. Vegetables

| | | |
|---|---|---|
| vegetables | **groenten** | ['xruntən] |
| greens | **verse kruiden** | ['vɛrsə 'krœʏdən] |
| | | |
| tomato | **tomaat (de)** | [tɔ'māt] |
| cucumber | **augurk (de)** | [au'xʉrk] |
| carrot | **wortel (de)** | ['wɔrtəl] |
| potato | **aardappel (de)** | ['ārd·apəl] |
| onion | **ui (de)** | ['œʏ] |
| garlic | **knoflook (de)** | ['knōflɔk] |
| | | |
| cabbage | **kool (de)** | [kōl] |
| cauliflower | **bloemkool (de)** | ['blum·kōl] |

| Brussels sprouts | spruitkool (de) | ['sprœyt·kōl] |
| broccoli | broccoli (de) | ['brɔkɔli] |

| beetroot | rode biet (de) | ['rɔdə bit] |
| eggplant | aubergine (de) | [ɔbɛr'ʒinə] |
| zucchini | courgette (de) | [kur'ʒɛt] |
| pumpkin | pompoen (de) | [pɔm'pun] |
| turnip | raap (de) | [rãp] |

| parsley | peterselie (de) | [petər'sɛli] |
| dill | dille (de) | ['dilə] |
| lettuce | sla (de) | [sla] |
| celery | selderij (de) | ['sɛldɛrɛj] |
| asparagus | asperge (de) | [as'pɛrʒə] |
| spinach | spinazie (de) | [spi'nazi] |

| pea | erwt (de) | [ɛrt] |
| beans | bonen | ['bonən] |
| corn (maize) | maïs (de) | [majs] |
| kidney bean | boon (de) | [bōn] |

| bell pepper | peper (de) | ['pepər] |
| radish | radijs (de) | [ra'dɛjs] |
| artichoke | artisjok (de) | [arti'ɕɔk] |

## 55. Fruits. Nuts

| fruit | vrucht (de) | [vrʊxt] |
| apple | appel (de) | ['apəl] |
| pear | peer (de) | [pēr] |
| lemon | citroen (de) | [si'trun] |
| orange | sinaasappel (de) | ['sinãsapəl] |
| strawberry (garden ~) | aardbei (de) | ['ãrd·bɛj] |

| mandarin | mandarijn (de) | [manda'rɛjn] |
| plum | pruim (de) | ['prœʏm] |
| peach | perzik (de) | ['pɛrzik] |
| apricot | abrikoos (de) | [abri'kōs] |
| raspberry | framboos (de) | [fram'bōs] |
| pineapple | ananas (de) | ['ananas] |

| banana | banaan (de) | [ba'nãn] |
| watermelon | watermeloen (de) | ['watərmɛ'lun] |
| grape | druif (de) | [drœʏf] |
| sour cherry | zure kers (de) | ['zʉrə kɛrs] |
| sweet cherry | zoete kers (de) | ['zutə kɛrs] |
| melon | meloen (de) | [mə'lun] |

| grapefruit | grapefruit (de) | ['grepfrut] |
| avocado | avocado (de) | [avɔ'kadɔ] |

| papaya | papaja (de) | [pa'paja] |
| mango | mango (de) | ['mangɔ] |
| pomegranate | granaatappel (de) | [xra'nāt·'apəl] |

| redcurrant | rode bes (de) | ['rɔdə bɛs] |
| blackcurrant | zwarte bes (de) | ['zwartə bɛs] |
| gooseberry | kruisbes (de) | ['krœʏsbɛs] |
| bilberry | bosbes (de) | ['bɔsbɛs] |
| blackberry | braambes (de) | ['brãmbɛs] |

| raisin | rozijn (de) | [rɔ'zɛjn] |
| fig | vijg (de) | [vɛjx] |
| date | dadel (de) | ['dadəl] |

| peanut | pinda (de) | ['pinda] |
| almond | amandel (de) | [a'mandəl] |
| walnut | walnoot (de) | ['walnõt] |
| hazelnut | hazelnoot (de) | ['hazəl·nõt] |
| coconut | kokosnoot (de) | ['kɔkɔs·nõt] |
| pistachios | pistaches | [pi'staʃəs] |

## 56. Bread. Candy

| bakers' confectionery (pastry) | suikerbakkerij (de) | [sœʏkər bakə'rɛj] |
| bread | brood (het) | [brõt] |
| cookies | koekje (het) | ['kukjə] |

| chocolate (n) | chocolade (de) | [ʃɔkɔ'ladə] |
| chocolate (as adj) | chocolade- | [ʃɔkɔ'ladə] |
| candy (wrapped) | snoepje (het) | ['snupjə] |
| cake (e.g., cupcake) | cakeje (het) | ['kejkjə] |
| cake (e.g., birthday ~) | taart (de) | [tãrt] |

| pie (e.g., apple ~) | pastei (de) | [pas'tɛj] |
| filling (for cake, pie) | vulling (de) | ['vʉliŋ] |

| jam (whole fruit jam) | confituur (de) | [kɔnfi'tūr] |
| marmalade | marmelade (de) | [marmə'ladə] |
| waffles | wafel (de) | ['wafəl] |
| ice-cream | ijsje (het) | ['ɛisjə], ['ɛiʃə] |
| pudding | pudding (de) | ['pʉdiŋ] |

## 57. Spices

| salt | zout (het) | ['zaut] |
| salty (adj) | gezouten | [xə'zautən] |
| to salt (vt) | zouten | ['zautən] |

| black pepper | zwarte peper (de) | ['zwartə 'pepər] |
| red pepper (milled ~) | rode peper (de) | ['rodə 'pepər] |
| mustard | mosterd (de) | ['mɔstərt] |
| horseradish | mierikswortel (de) | ['miriks·'wɔrtəl] |

| condiment | condiment (het) | [kɔndi'mɛnt] |
| spice | specerij , kruiderij (de) | [spesə'rɛj], [krœʏdə'rɛj] |
| sauce | saus (de) | ['saus] |
| vinegar | azijn (de) | [a'zɛjn] |

| anise | anijs (de) | [a'nɛjs] |
| basil | basilicum (de) | [ba'silikəm] |
| cloves | kruidnagel (de) | ['krœʏtnaxəl] |
| ginger | gember (de) | ['xɛmbər] |
| coriander | koriander (de) | [kɔri'andər] |
| cinnamon | kaneel (de/het) | [ka'nēl] |

| sesame | sesamzaad (het) | ['sɛzam·zāt] |
| bay leaf | laurierblad (het) | [lau'rir·blat] |
| paprika | paprika (de) | ['paprika] |
| caraway | komijn (de) | [kɔ'mɛjn] |
| saffron | saffraan (de) | [saf'rān] |

T&P BOOKS

# PERSONAL
# INFORMATION. FAMILY

T&P Books Publishing

| | | |
|---|---|---|
| name (first name) | **naam (de)** | [nām] |
| surname (last name) | **achternaam (de)** | ['axtər·nām] |
| date of birth | **geboortedatum (de)** | [xə'bŏrtə·datʉm] |
| place of birth | **geboorteplaats (de)** | [xə'bŏrtə·plāts] |
| | | |
| nationality | **nationaliteit (de)** | [natsjɔnali'tɛjt] |
| place of residence | **woonplaats (de)** | ['wŏm·plāts] |
| country | **land (het)** | [lant] |
| profession (occupation) | **beroep (het)** | [bə'rup] |
| | | |
| gender, sex | **geslacht (het)** | [xə'slaht] |
| height | **lengte (de)** | ['lɛŋtə] |
| weight | **gewicht (het)** | [xə'wixt] |

| | | |
|---|---|---|
| mother | **moeder (de)** | ['mudər] |
| father | **vader (de)** | ['vadər] |
| son | **zoon (de)** | [zŏn] |
| daughter | **dochter (de)** | ['dɔxtər] |
| | | |
| younger daughter | **jongste dochter (de)** | ['joŋstə 'dɔxtər] |
| younger son | **jongste zoon (de)** | ['joŋstə zŏn] |
| eldest daughter | **oudste dochter (de)** | ['audstə 'dɔxtər] |
| eldest son | **oudste zoon (de)** | ['audstə zŏn] |
| | | |
| brother | **broer (de)** | [brur] |
| elder brother | **oudere broer (de)** | ['audərə brur] |
| younger brother | **jongere broer (de)** | ['joŋərə brur] |
| sister | **zuster (de)** | ['zʉstər] |
| elder sister | **oudere zuster (de)** | ['audərə 'zʉstər] |
| younger sister | **jongere zuster (de)** | ['joŋərə 'zʉstər] |
| | | |
| cousin (masc.) | **neef (de)** | [nĕf] |
| cousin (fem.) | **nicht (de)** | [nixt] |
| mom, mommy | **mama (de)** | ['mama] |
| dad, daddy | **papa (de)** | ['papa] |
| parents | **ouders** | ['audərs] |
| child | **kind (het)** | [kint] |
| children | **kinderen** | ['kindərən] |
| grandmother | **oma (de)** | ['ɔma] |
| grandfather | **opa (de)** | ['ɔpa] |

| | | |
|---|---|---|
| grandson | **kleinzoon (de)** | [klɛjn·zõn] |
| granddaughter | **kleindochter (de)** | [klɛjn·'dɔxtər] |
| grandchildren | **kleinkinderen** | [klɛjn·'kinderən] |
| | | |
| uncle | **oom (de)** | [õm] |
| aunt | **tante (de)** | ['tantə] |
| nephew | **neef (de)** | [nẽf] |
| niece | **nicht (de)** | [nixt] |
| | | |
| mother-in-law (wife's mother) | **schoonmoeder (de)** | ['sxõn·mudər] |
| father-in-law (husband's father) | **schoonvader (de)** | ['sxõn·vadər] |
| son-in-law (daughter's husband) | **schoonzoon (de)** | ['sxõn·zõn] |
| stepmother | **stiefmoeder (de)** | ['stif·mudər] |
| stepfather | **stiefvader (de)** | ['stif·vadər] |
| | | |
| infant | **zuigeling (de)** | ['zœɣxəliŋ] |
| baby (infant) | **wiegenkind (het)** | ['wixən·kint] |
| little boy, kid | **kleuter (de)** | ['kløtər] |
| | | |
| wife | **vrouw (de)** | ['vrau] |
| husband | **man (de)** | [man] |
| spouse (husband) | **echtgenoot (de)** | ['ɛhtxənõt] |
| spouse (wife) | **echtgenote (de)** | ['ɛhtxənɔtə] |
| | | |
| married (masc.) | **gehuwd** | [xə'hʉwt] |
| married (fem.) | **gehuwd** | [xə'hʉwt] |
| single (unmarried) | **ongehuwd** | [ɔnhə'hʉwt] |
| bachelor | **vrijgezel (de)** | [vrɛjxə'zɛl] |
| divorced (masc.) | **gescheiden** | [xə'sxɛjdən] |
| widow | **weduwe (de)** | ['wedʉwə] |
| widower | **weduwnaar (de)** | ['wedʉwnãr] |
| | | |
| relative | **familielid (het)** | [fa'mililit] |
| close relative | **dichte familielid (het)** | ['dixtə fa'mililit] |
| distant relative | **verre familielid (het)** | ['vɛrə fa'mililit] |
| relatives | **familieleden** | [fa'mili'ledən] |
| | | |
| orphan (boy or girl) | **wees (de), weeskind (het)** | [wẽs], ['wẽskint] |
| guardian (of a minor) | **voogd (de)** | [võxt] |
| to adopt (a boy) | **adopteren** | [adɔp'terən] |
| to adopt (a girl) | **adopteren** | [adɔp'terən] |

## 60. Friends. Coworkers

| | | |
|---|---|---|
| friend (masc.) | **vriend (de)** | [vrint] |
| friend (fem.) | **vriendin (de)** | [vrin'din] |

| friendship | vriendschap (de) | ['vrintsxap] |
| to be friends | bevriend zijn | [bə'vrint zɛjn] |

| buddy (masc.) | makker (de) | ['makər] |
| buddy (fem.) | vriendin (de) | [vrin'din] |
| partner | partner (de) | ['partnər] |

| chief (boss) | chef (de) | [ʃɛf] |
| superior (n) | baas (de) | [bās] |
| owner, proprietor | eigenaar (de) | ['ɛjxənār] |
| subordinate (n) | ondergeschikte (de) | ['ɔndərxə'sxiktə] |
| colleague | collega (de) | [kɔ'lexa] |

| acquaintance (person) | kennis (de) | ['kɛnis] |
| fellow traveler | medereiziger (de) | ['medə·'rɛjzixər] |
| classmate | klasgenoot (de) | ['klas·xənōt] |

| neighbor (masc.) | buurman (de) | ['būrman] |
| neighbor (fem.) | buurvrouw (de) | ['būrvrau] |
| neighbors | buren | ['bʉrən] |

# HUMAN BODY.
# MEDICINE

**T&P Books Publishing**

## 61. Head

| | | |
|---|---|---|
| head | hoofd (het) | [hõft] |
| face | gezicht (het) | [xə'ziht] |
| nose | neus (de) | ['nøs] |
| mouth | mond (de) | [mɔnt] |

| | | |
|---|---|---|
| eye | oog (het) | [õx] |
| eyes | ogen | ['ɔxən] |
| pupil | pupil (de) | [pʉ'pil] |
| eyebrow | wenkbrauw (de) | ['wɛnk·brau] |
| eyelash | wimper (de) | ['wimpər] |
| eyelid | ooglid (het) | ['õx·lit] |

| | | |
|---|---|---|
| tongue | tong (de) | [tɔŋ] |
| tooth | tand (de) | [tant] |
| lips | lippen | ['lipən] |
| cheekbones | jukbeenderen | [juk'·bẽndərən] |
| gum | tandvlees (het) | ['tand·vlẽs] |
| palate | gehemelte (het) | [xə'heməltə] |

| | | |
|---|---|---|
| nostrils | neusgaten | ['nøsxatən] |
| chin | kin (de) | [kin] |
| jaw | kaak (de) | [kãk] |
| cheek | wang (de) | [waŋ] |

| | | |
|---|---|---|
| forehead | voorhoofd (het) | ['võrhõft] |
| temple | slaap (de) | [slãp] |
| ear | oor (het) | [õr] |
| back of the head | achterhoofd (het) | ['axtər·hõft] |
| neck | hals (de) | [hals] |
| throat | keel (de) | [kẽl] |

| | | |
|---|---|---|
| hair | haren | ['harən] |
| hairstyle | kapsel (het) | ['kapsəl] |
| haircut | haarsnit (de) | ['hãrsnit] |
| wig | pruik (de) | ['prœʏk] |

| | | |
|---|---|---|
| mustache | snor (de) | [snɔr] |
| beard | baard (de) | [bãrt] |
| to have (a beard, etc.) | dragen | ['draxən] |
| braid | vlecht (de) | [vlɛxt] |
| sideburns | bakkebaarden | [bakə'bãrtən] |

| | | |
|---|---|---|
| red-haired (adj) | ros | [rɔs] |
| gray (hair) | grijs | [xrɛjs] |

| bald (adj) | **kaal** | [kāl] |
| bald patch | **kale plek (de)** | ['kalə plɛk] |
| | | |
| ponytail | **paardenstaart (de)** | ['pārdən·stārt] |
| bangs | **pony (de)** | ['pɔni] |

## 62. Human body

| hand | **hand (de)** | [hant] |
| arm | **arm (de)** | [arm] |
| | | |
| finger | **vinger (de)** | ['viŋər] |
| toe | **teen (de)** | [tēn] |
| thumb | **duim (de)** | ['dœʏm] |
| little finger | **pink (de)** | [pink] |
| nail | **nagel (de)** | ['naxəl] |
| | | |
| fist | **vuist (de)** | ['vœʏst] |
| palm | **handpalm (de)** | ['hantpalm] |
| wrist | **pols (de)** | [pɔls] |
| forearm | **voorarm (de)** | ['vōrarm] |
| elbow | **elleboog (de)** | ['ɛləbōx] |
| shoulder | **schouder (de)** | ['sxaudər] |
| | | |
| leg | **been (het)** | [bēn] |
| foot | **voet (de)** | [vut] |
| knee | **knie (de)** | [kni] |
| calf (part of leg) | **kuit (de)** | ['kœʏt] |
| hip | **heup (de)** | ['høp] |
| heel | **hiel (de)** | [hil] |
| | | |
| body | **lichaam (het)** | ['lixām] |
| stomach | **buik (de)** | ['bœʏk] |
| chest | **borst (de)** | [bɔrst] |
| breast | **borst (de)** | [bɔrst] |
| flank | **zijde (de)** | ['zɛjdə] |
| back | **rug (de)** | [rʉx] |
| | | |
| lower back | **lage rug (de)** | [laxə rʉx] |
| waist | **taille (de)** | ['tajə] |
| | | |
| navel (belly button) | **navel (de)** | ['navəl] |
| buttocks | **billen** | ['bilən] |
| bottom | **achterwerk (het)** | ['axtərwɛrk] |
| | | |
| beauty mark | **huidvlek (de)** | ['hœʏt·vlɛk] |
| birthmark | **moedervlek (de)** | ['mudər·vlɛk] |
| (café au lait spot) | | |
| tattoo | **tatoeage (de)** | [tatu'aʒə] |
| scar | **litteken (het)** | ['litekən] |

## 63. Diseases

| | | |
|---|---|---|
| sickness | ziekte (de) | ['ziktə] |
| to be sick | ziek zijn | [zik zɛjn] |
| health | gezondheid (de) | [xə'zɔnthɛjt] |
| | | |
| runny nose (coryza) | snotneus (de) | [snɔt'nøs] |
| tonsillitis | angina (de) | [an'xina] |
| cold (illness) | verkoudheid (de) | [vər'kauthɛjt] |
| to catch a cold | verkouden raken | [vər'kaudən 'rakən] |
| | | |
| bronchitis | bronchitis (de) | [brɔn'xitis] |
| pneumonia | longontsteking (de) | ['lɔŋ·ɔntstekiŋ] |
| flu, influenza | griep (de) | [xrip] |
| | | |
| nearsighted (adj) | bijziend | [bɛj'zint] |
| farsighted (adj) | verziend | ['vɛrzint] |
| strabismus (crossed eyes) | scheelheid (de) | ['sxēlxɛjt] |
| cross-eyed (adj) | scheel | [sxēl] |
| cataract | grauwe staar (de) | ['xrauə stār] |
| glaucoma | glaucoom (het) | [xlau'kōm] |
| | | |
| stroke | beroerte (de) | [bə'rurtə] |
| heart attack | hartinfarct (het) | ['hart·in'farkt] |
| myocardial infarction | myocardiaal infarct (het) | [miɔkardi'āl in'farkt] |
| paralysis | verlamming (de) | [vər'lamiŋ] |
| to paralyze (vt) | verlammen | [vər'lamən] |
| | | |
| allergy | allergie (de) | [alɛr'xi] |
| asthma | astma (de/het) | ['astma] |
| diabetes | diabetes (de) | [dia'betəs] |
| | | |
| toothache | tandpijn (de) | ['tand·pɛjn] |
| caries | tandbederf (het) | ['tand·bə'dɛrf] |
| | | |
| diarrhea | diarree (de) | [dia'rē] |
| constipation | constipatie (de) | [kɔnsti'patsi] |
| stomach upset | maagstoornis (de) | ['māx·stōrnis] |
| food poisoning | voedselvergiftiging (de) | ['vudsəl·vər'xiftəxiŋ] |
| to get food poisoning | voedselvergiftiging oplopen | ['vudsəl·vər'xiftəxiŋ 'ɔplɔpən] |
| | | |
| arthritis | artritis (de) | [ar'tritis] |
| rickets | rachitis (de) | [ra'xitis] |
| rheumatism | reuma (het) | ['røma] |
| atherosclerosis | arteriosclerose (de) | [artɛriɔskle'rɔzə] |
| | | |
| gastritis | gastritis (de) | [xas'tritis] |
| appendicitis | blindedarm- montsteking (de) | [blində'darm ɔntstekiŋ] |
| cholecystitis | galblaasontsteking (de) | ['xalblaxāns·ɔnt'stekiŋ] |

| | | |
|---|---|---|
| ulcer | zweer (de) | [zwēr] |
| measles | mazelen | ['mazelən] |
| rubella (German measles) | rodehond (de) | ['rodəhont] |
| jaundice | geelzucht (de) | ['xēlzʉht] |
| hepatitis | leverontsteking (de) | ['levər ɔnt'stekiŋ] |
| | | |
| schizophrenia | schizofrenie (de) | [sxitsɔfrə'ni] |
| rabies (hydrophobia) | dolheid (de) | ['dɔlhɛjt] |
| neurosis | neurose (de) | ['nø'rozə] |
| concussion | hersenschudding (de) | ['hɛrsən·sxjudiŋ] |
| | | |
| cancer | kanker (de) | ['kankər] |
| sclerosis | sclerose (de) | [skle'rɔzə] |
| multiple sclerosis | multiple sclerose (de) | ['mʉltiplə skle'rɔzə] |
| | | |
| alcoholism | alcoholisme (het) | [alkɔhɔ'lismə] |
| alcoholic (n) | alcoholicus (de) | [alkɔ'hɔlikʉs] |
| syphilis | syfilis (de) | ['sifilis] |
| AIDS | AIDS (de) | [ets] |
| | | |
| tumor | tumor (de) | ['tʉmɔr] |
| malignant (adj) | kwaadaardig | ['kwāt·'ārdəx] |
| benign (adj) | goedaardig | [xu'tārdəx] |
| | | |
| fever | koorts (de) | [kōrts] |
| malaria | malaria (de) | [ma'laria] |
| gangrene | gangreen (het) | [xanx'rēn] |
| seasickness | zeeziekte (de) | [zē·'ziktə] |
| epilepsy | epilepsie (de) | [ɛpilɛp'si] |
| | | |
| epidemic | epidemie (de) | [ɛpidə'mi] |
| typhus | tyfus (de) | ['tifʉs] |
| tuberculosis | tuberculose (de) | [tʉbərkʉ'lɔzə] |
| cholera | cholera (de) | ['xɔlera] |
| plague (bubonic ~) | pest (de) | [pɛst] |

## 64. Symptoms. Treatments. Part 1

| | | |
|---|---|---|
| symptom | symptoom (het) | [simp'tōm] |
| temperature | temperatuur (de) | [tɛmpəra'tūr] |
| high temperature (fever) | verhoogde temperatuur (de) | [vər'hōxtə tɛmpəra'tūr] |
| pulse | polsslag (de) | ['pɔls·slax] |
| | | |
| dizziness (vertigo) | duizeling (de) | ['dœyzəliŋ] |
| hot (adj) | heet | [hēt] |
| shivering | koude rillingen | ['kaudə 'riliŋən] |
| pale (e.g., ~ face) | bleek | [blēk] |
| cough | hoest (de) | [hust] |
| to cough (vi) | hoesten | ['hustən] |

| | | |
|---|---|---|
| to sneeze (vi) | niezen | ['nizən] |
| faint | flauwte (de) | ['flautə] |
| to faint (vi) | flauwvallen | ['flauvalən] |

| | | |
|---|---|---|
| bruise (hématome) | blauwe plek (de) | ['blauə plɛk] |
| bump (lump) | buil (de) | ['bœʏl] |
| to bang (bump) | zich stoten | [zix 'stɔtən] |
| contusion (bruise) | kneuzing (de) | ['knøziŋ] |
| to get a bruise | kneuzen | ['knøzən] |

| | | |
|---|---|---|
| to limp (vi) | hinken | ['hinkən] |
| dislocation | verstuiking (de) | [vər'stœʏkiŋ] |
| to dislocate (vt) | verstuiken | [vər'stœʏkən] |
| fracture | breuk (de) | ['brøk] |
| to have a fracture | een breuk oplopen | [en 'brøk 'ɔplɔpən] |

| | | |
|---|---|---|
| cut (e.g., paper ~) | snijwond (de) | ['snɛj·wɔnt] |
| to cut oneself | zich snijden | [zix snɛjdən] |
| bleeding | bloeding (de) | ['bludiŋ] |

| | | |
|---|---|---|
| burn (injury) | brandwond (de) | ['brant·wɔnt] |
| to get burned | zich branden | [zix 'brandən] |

| | | |
|---|---|---|
| to prick (vt) | prikken | ['prikən] |
| to prick oneself | zich prikken | [zix 'prikən] |
| to injure (vt) | blesseren | [blɛ'serən] |
| injury | blessure (de) | [blɛ'sʉrə] |
| wound | wond (de) | [wɔnt] |
| trauma | trauma (het) | ['trauma] |

| | | |
|---|---|---|
| to be delirious | ijlen | ['ɛjlən] |
| to stutter (vi) | stotteren | ['stɔtɛrən] |
| sunstroke | zonnesteek (de) | ['zɔnə·stẽk] |

## 65. Symptoms. Treatments. Part 2

| | | |
|---|---|---|
| pain, ache | pijn (de) | [pɛjn] |
| splinter (in foot, etc.) | splinter (de) | ['splintər] |

| | | |
|---|---|---|
| sweat (perspiration) | zweet (het) | ['zwẽt] |
| to sweat (perspire) | zweten | ['zwetən] |
| vomiting | braking (de) | ['brakiŋ] |
| convulsions | stuiptrekkingen | ['stœʏp·'trɛkiŋən] |

| | | |
|---|---|---|
| pregnant (adj) | zwanger | ['zwaŋər] |
| to be born | geboren worden | [xə'bɔrən 'wɔrdən] |
| delivery, labor | geboorte (de) | [xə'bõrtə] |
| to deliver (~ a baby) | baren | ['barən] |
| abortion | abortus (de) | [a'bɔrtus] |
| breathing, respiration | ademhaling (de) | ['adəmhaliŋ] |

| in-breath (inhalation) | inademing (de) | ['inademiŋ] |
| out-breath (exhalation) | uitademing (de) | ['œʏtademiŋ] |
| to exhale (breathe out) | uitademen | ['œʏtademən] |
| to inhale (vi) | inademen | ['inademən] |

| disabled person | invalide (de) | [inva'lidə] |
| cripple | gehandicapte (de) | [hə'handikaptə] |
| drug addict | drugsverslaafde (de) | ['drʉks·vər'slãfdə] |

| deaf (adj) | doof | [dõf] |
| mute (adj) | stom | [stɔm] |
| deaf mute (adj) | doofstom | [dõf·'stɔm] |

| mad, insane (adj) | krankzinnig | [kraŋk'sinəx] |
| madman (demented person) | krankzinnige (de) | [kraŋk'sinəxə] |
| madwoman | krankzinnige (de) | [kraŋk'sinəxə] |
| to go insane | krankzinnig worden | [kraŋk'sinəx 'wɔrdən] |

| gene | gen (het) | [xen] |
| immunity | immuniteit (de) | [imʉni'tɛjt] |
| hereditary (adj) | erfelijk | ['ɛrfələk] |
| congenital (adj) | aangeboren | ['ãnxəborən] |

| virus | virus (het) | ['virʉs] |
| microbe | microbe (de) | [mik'robə] |
| bacterium | bacterie (de) | [bak'teri] |
| infection | infectie (de) | [in'fɛksi] |

## 66. Symptoms. Treatments. Part 3

| hospital | ziekenhuis (het) | ['zikən·hœʏs] |
| patient | patiènt (de) | [pasi'ent] |

| diagnosis | diagnose (de) | [diax'nɔzə] |
| cure | genezing (de) | [xə'nezin] |
| medical treatment | medische behandeling (de) | ['mɛdisə bə'handəliŋ] |

| to get treatment | onder behandeling zijn | ['ɔndər bə'handəliŋ zɛjn] |
| to treat (~ a patient) | behandelen | [bə'handələn] |
| to nurse (look after) | zorgen | ['zɔrxən] |
| care (nursing ~) | ziekenzorg (de) | ['zikən·zɔrx] |

| operation, surgery | operatie (de) | [ɔpe'ratsi] |
| to bandage (head, limb) | verbinden | [vər'bindən] |
| bandaging | verband (het) | [vər'bant] |

| vaccination | vaccin (het) | [vaksən] |
| to vaccinate (vt) | inenten | ['inɛntən] |
| injection, shot | injectie (de) | [inj'eksi] |

| | | |
|---|---|---|
| to give an injection | **een injectie geven** | [ɛn inj'eksi 'xɛvən] |
| attack | **aanval (de)** | ['ānval] |
| amputation | **amputatie (de)** | [ampʉ'tatsi] |
| to amputate (vt) | **amputeren** | [ampʉ'terən] |
| coma | **coma (het)** | ['kɔma] |
| to be in a coma | **in coma liggen** | [in 'kɔma 'lixən] |
| intensive care | **intensieve zorg, ICU (de)** | [intən'sivə zɔrx], [isɛ'ju] |
| | | |
| to recover (~ from flu) | **zich herstellen** | [zix hɛr'ʃtɛlən] |
| condition (patient's ~) | **toestand (de)** | ['tustant] |
| consciousness | **bewustzijn (het)** | [bə'wʉstsɛjn] |
| memory (faculty) | **geheugen (het)** | [xə'høxən] |
| | | |
| to pull out (tooth) | **trekken** | ['trɛkən] |
| filling | **vulling (de)** | ['vʉliŋ] |
| to fill (a tooth) | **vullen** | ['vʉlən] |
| | | |
| hypnosis | **hypnose (de)** | ['hipnɔzə] |
| to hypnotize (vt) | **hypnotiseren** | [hipnɔti'zerən] |

## 67. Medicine. Drugs. Accessories

| | | |
|---|---|---|
| medicine, drug | **geneesmiddel (het)** | [xə'nēsmidəl] |
| remedy | **middel (het)** | ['midəl] |
| to prescribe (vt) | **voorschrijven** | ['vōrsxrɛjvən] |
| prescription | **recept (het)** | [re'sɛpt] |
| | | |
| tablet, pill | **tablet (de/het)** | [tab'lɛt] |
| ointment | **zalf (de)** | [zalf] |
| ampule | **ampul (de)** | [am'pʉl] |
| mixture | **drank (de)** | [drank] |
| syrup | **siroop (de)** | [si'rōp] |
| pill | **pil (de)** | [pil] |
| powder | **poeder (de/het)** | ['pudər] |
| | | |
| gauze bandage | **verband (het)** | [vər'bant] |
| cotton wool | **watten** | ['watən] |
| iodine | **jodium (het)** | ['jodijum] |
| | | |
| Band-Aid | **pleister (de)** | ['plɛjstər] |
| eyedropper | **pipet (de)** | [pi'pɛt] |
| thermometer | **thermometer (de)** | ['tɛrmɔmetər] |
| syringe | **spuit (de)** | ['spœyt] |
| | | |
| wheelchair | **rolstoel (de)** | ['rɔl·stul] |
| crutches | **krukken** | ['krʉkən] |
| | | |
| painkiller | **pijnstiller (de)** | ['pɛjn·stilər] |
| laxative | **laxeermiddel (het)** | [la'ksēr·midəl] |
| spirits (ethanol) | **spiritus (de)** | ['spiritʉs] |

| medicinal herbs | **medicinale kruiden** | [mɛdisi'nalə krœʏdən] |
| herbal (~ tea) | **kruiden-** | ['krœʏdən] |

BOOKS

# APARTMENT

**T&P Books Publishing**

## 68. Apartment

| | | |
|---|---|---|
| apartment | **appartement (het)** | [apartə'mɛnt] |
| room | **kamer (de)** | ['kamər] |
| bedroom | **slaapkamer (de)** | ['slāp·kamər] |
| dining room | **eetkamer (de)** | [ēt·'kamər] |
| living room | **salon (de)** | [sa'lɔn] |
| study (home office) | **studeerkamer (de)** | [stu'dēr·'kamər] |
| | | |
| entry room | **gang (de)** | [xaŋ] |
| bathroom (room with a bath or shower) | **badkamer (de)** | ['bat·kamər] |
| half bath | **toilet (het)** | [tua'lɛt] |
| | | |
| ceiling | **plafond (het)** | [pla'fɔnt] |
| floor | **vloer (de)** | [vlur] |
| corner | **hoek (de)** | [huk] |

## 69. Furniture. Interior

| | | |
|---|---|---|
| furniture | **meubels** | ['møbəl] |
| table | **tafel (de)** | ['tafəl] |
| chair | **stoel (de)** | [stul] |
| bed | **bed (het)** | [bɛt] |
| couch, sofa | **bankstel (het)** | ['bankstəl] |
| armchair | **fauteuil (de)** | [fɔ'tøj] |
| | | |
| bookcase | **boekenkast (de)** | ['bukən·kast] |
| shelf | **boekenrek (het)** | ['bukən·rɛk] |
| | | |
| wardrobe | **kledingkast (de)** | ['klediŋ·kast] |
| coat rack (wall-mounted ~) | **kapstok (de)** | ['kapstɔk] |
| coat stand | **staande kapstok (de)** | ['stāndə 'kapstɔk] |
| | | |
| bureau, dresser | **commode (de)** | [kɔ'mɔdə] |
| coffee table | **salontafeltje (het)** | [sa'lɔn·'tafəltʃə] |
| | | |
| mirror | **spiegel (de)** | ['spixəl] |
| carpet | **tapijt (het)** | [ta'pɛjt] |
| rug, small carpet | **tapijtje (het)** | [ta'pɛjtʃə] |
| | | |
| fireplace | **haard (de)** | [hārt] |
| candle | **kaars (de)** | [kārs] |
| candlestick | **kandelaar (de)** | ['kandəlār] |

| drapes | gordijnen | [xɔr'dɛjnən] |
| wallpaper | behang (het) | [bə'haŋ] |
| blinds (jalousie) | jaloezie (de) | [jalu'zi] |

| table lamp | bureaulamp (de) | [bʉ'rɔ·lamp] |
| wall lamp (sconce) | wandlamp (de) | ['want·lamp] |
| floor lamp | staande lamp (de) | ['stāndə lamp] |
| chandelier | luchter (de) | ['lʉxtər] |

| leg (of chair, table) | poot (de) | [pōt] |
| armrest | armleuning (de) | [arm·'løniŋ] |
| back (backrest) | rugleuning (de) | ['rʉx·'løniŋ] |
| drawer | la (de) | [la] |

## 70. Bedding

| bedclothes | beddengoed (het) | ['bɛdən·xut] |
| pillow | kussen (het) | ['kʉsən] |
| pillowcase | kussenovertrek (de) | ['kʉsən·'ɔvərtrɛk] |
| duvet, comforter | deken (de) | ['dekən] |
| sheet | laken (het) | ['lakən] |
| bedspread | sprei (de) | [sprɛj] |

## 71. Kitchen

| kitchen | keuken (de) | ['køkən] |
| gas | gas (het) | [xas] |
| gas stove (range) | gasfornuis (het) | [xas·fɔr'nœys] |
| electric stove | elektrisch fornuis (het) | [ɛ'lɛktris fɔr'nœys] |
| oven | oven (de) | ['ɔvən] |
| microwave oven | magnetronoven (de) | ['mahnətrɔn·'ɔvən] |

| refrigerator | koelkast (de) | ['kul·kast] |
| freezer | diepvriezer (de) | [dip·'vrizər] |
| dishwasher | vaatwasmachine (de) | ['vātwas·ma'ʃinə] |

| meat grinder | vleesmolen (de) | ['vlēs·mɔlən] |
| juicer | vruchtenpers (de) | ['vrʉxtən·pɛrs] |
| toaster | toaster (de) | ['tōstər] |
| mixer | mixer (de) | ['miksər] |

| coffee machine | koffiemachine (de) | ['kɔfi·ma'ʃinə] |
| coffee pot | koffiepot (de) | ['kɔfi·pot] |
| coffee grinder | koffiemolen (de) | ['kɔfi·mɔlən] |

| kettle | fluitketel (de) | ['flœyt·'ketəl] |
| teapot | theepot (de) | ['tē·pot] |
| lid | deksel (de/het) | ['dɛksəl] |

| tea strainer | theezeefje (het) | ['tē·zefjə] |
| spoon | lepel (de) | ['lepəl] |
| teaspoon | theelepeltje (het) | [tē·'lepəltʃə] |
| soup spoon | eetlepel (de) | [ēt·'lepəl] |
| fork | vork (de) | [vɔrk] |
| knife | mes (het) | [mɛs] |

| tableware (dishes) | vaatwerk (het) | ['vātwɛrk] |
| plate (dinner ~) | bord (het) | [bɔrt] |
| saucer | schoteltje (het) | ['sxɔteltʃə] |

| shot glass | likeurglas (het) | [li'kør·xlas] |
| glass (tumbler) | glas (het) | [xlas] |
| cup | kopje (het) | ['kɔpjə] |

| sugar bowl | suikerpot (de) | [sœykər·pɔt] |
| salt shaker | zoutvat (het) | ['zaut·vat] |
| pepper shaker | pepervat (het) | ['pepər·vat] |
| butter dish | boterschaaltje (het) | ['botər·'sxāltʃe] |

| stock pot (soup pot) | pan (de) | [pan] |
| frying pan (skillet) | bakpan (de) | ['bak·pan] |
| ladle | pollepel (de) | [pɔl·'lepəl] |
| colander | vergiet (de/het) | [vər'xit] |
| tray (serving ~) | dienblad (het) | ['dinblat] |

| bottle | fles (de) | [fles] |
| jar (glass) | glazen pot (de) | ['xlazən pɔt] |
| can | blik (het) | [blik] |

| bottle opener | flesopener (de) | [fles·'ɔpənər] |
| can opener | blikopener (de) | [blik·'ɔpənər] |
| corkscrew | kurkentrekker (de) | ['kurkən·'trɛkər] |
| filter | filter (de/het) | ['filtər] |
| to filter (vt) | filteren | ['filtərən] |

| trash, garbage (food waste, etc.) | huisvuil (het) | ['hœʏsvœʏl] |
| trash can (kitchen ~) | vuilnisemmer (de) | ['vœʏlnis·'ɛmər] |

## 72. Bathroom

| bathroom | badkamer (de) | ['bat·kamər] |
| water | water (het) | ['watər] |
| faucet | kraan (de) | [krān] |
| hot water | warm water (het) | [warm 'watər] |
| cold water | koud water (het) | ['kaut 'watər] |

| toothpaste | tandpasta (de) | ['tand·pasta] |
| to brush one's teeth | tanden poetsen | ['tandən 'putsən] |

| | | |
|---|---|---|
| toothbrush | tandenborstel (de) | ['tandən·'bɔrstəl] |
| to shave (vi) | zich scheren | [zix 'sxerən] |
| shaving foam | scheercrème (de) | [sxēr·krɛ:m] |
| razor | scheermes (het) | ['sxēr·mɛs] |
| | | |
| to wash (one's hands, etc.) | wassen | ['wasən] |
| to take a bath | een bad nemen | [en bat 'nemən] |
| shower | douche (de) | [duʃ] |
| to take a shower | een douche nemen | [en duʃ 'nemən] |
| | | |
| bathtub | bad (het) | [bat] |
| toilet (toilet bowl) | toiletpot (de) | [tua'lɛt·pɔt] |
| sink (washbasin) | wastafel (de) | ['was·tafəl] |
| | | |
| soap | zeep (de) | [zēp] |
| soap dish | zeepbakje (het) | ['zēp·bakjə] |
| | | |
| sponge | spons (de) | [spɔns] |
| shampoo | shampoo (de) | ['ʃʌmpō] |
| towel | handdoek (de) | ['handuk] |
| bathrobe | badjas (de) | ['batjas] |
| | | |
| laundry (process) | was (de) | [was] |
| washing machine | wasmachine (de) | ['was·ma'ʃinə] |
| to do the laundry | de was doen | [də was dun] |
| laundry detergent | waspoeder (de) | ['was·'pudər] |

## 73. Household appliances

| | | |
|---|---|---|
| TV set | televisie (de) | [telə'vizi] |
| tape recorder | cassettespeler (de) | [ka'sɛtə·'spelər] |
| VCR (video recorder) | videorecorder (de) | ['video·re'kɔrdər] |
| radio | radio (de) | ['radiɔ] |
| player (CD, MP3, etc.) | speler (de) | ['spelər] |
| | | |
| video projector | videoprojector (de) | ['video·prɔ'jektɔr] |
| home movie theater | home theater systeem (het) | [hɔm te'jatər si'stēm] |
| DVD player | DVD-speler (de) | [deve'de-'spelər] |
| amplifier | versterker (de) | [vər'stɛrkər] |
| video game console | spelconsole (de) | ['spɛl·kɔn'sɔlə] |
| | | |
| video camera | videocamera (de) | ['video·'kaməra] |
| camera (photo) | fotocamera (de) | ['foto·'kaməra] |
| digital camera | digitale camera (de) | [dixi'talə 'kaməra] |
| | | |
| vacuum cleaner | stofzuiger (de) | ['stɔf·zœyxər] |
| iron (e.g., steam ~) | strijkijzer (het) | ['strɛjk·ɛjzər] |
| ironing board | strijkplank (de) | ['strɛjk·plank] |
| telephone | telefoon (de) | [telə'fōn] |

| cell phone | **mobieltje (het)** | [mɔ'biltʃe] |
| typewriter | **schrijfmachine (de)** | ['sxrɛjf·ma'ʃine] |
| sewing machine | **naaimachine (de)** | ['nāj·ma'ʃine] |

| microphone | **microfoon (de)** | [mikrɔ'fōn] |
| headphones | **koptelefoon (de)** | ['kɔp·tele'fōn] |
| remote control (TV) | **afstandsbediening (de)** | ['afstants·be'diniŋ] |

| CD, compact disc | **CD (de)** | [se'de] |
| cassette, tape | **cassette (de)** | [ka'sɛte] |
| vinyl record | **vinylplaat (de)** | [vi'nil·plāt] |

T&P BOOKS

# THE EARTH. WEATHER

T&P Books Publishing

| space | kosmos (de) | ['kɔsmɔs] |
| space (as adj) | kosmisch | ['kɔsmis] |
| outer space | kosmische ruimte (de) | ['kɔsmisə 'rœʏmtə] |
| | | |
| world | wereld (de) | ['werəlt] |
| universe | heelal (het) | [hē'lal] |
| galaxy | sterrenstelsel (het) | ['stɛrən·'stɛlsəl] |
| | | |
| star | ster (de) | [stɛr] |
| constellation | sterrenbeeld (het) | ['stɛrən·bēlt] |
| planet | planeet (de) | [pla'nēt] |
| satellite | satelliet (de) | [satə'lit] |
| | | |
| meteorite | meteoriet (de) | [meteɔ'rit] |
| comet | komeet (de) | [kɔ'mēt] |
| asteroid | asteroïde (de) | [aste'rɔidə] |
| | | |
| orbit | baan (de) | [bān] |
| to revolve | draaien | ['drājən] |
| (~ around the Earth) | | |
| atmosphere | atmosfeer (de) | [atmɔ'sfēr] |
| | | |
| the Sun | Zon (de) | [zɔn] |
| solar system | zonnestelsel (het) | ['zɔnə·stɛlsəl] |
| solar eclipse | zonsverduistering (de) | ['zɔns·vər'dœʏsteriŋ] |
| | | |
| the Earth | Aarde (de) | ['ārdə] |
| the Moon | Maan (de) | [mān] |
| | | |
| Mars | Mars (de) | [mars] |
| Venus | Venus (de) | ['venʉs] |
| Jupiter | Jupiter (de) | [jupi'tɛr] |
| Saturn | Saturnus (de) | [sa'tʉrnʉs] |
| | | |
| Mercury | Mercurius (de) | [mər'kʉrijus] |
| Uranus | Uranus (de) | [u'ranʉs] |
| Neptune | Neptunus (de) | [nep'tʉnʉs] |
| Pluto | Pluto (de) | ['plʉtɔ] |
| | | |
| Milky Way | Melkweg (de) | ['mɛlk·wɛx] |
| Great Bear (Ursa Major) | Grote Beer (de) | ['xrɔtə bēr] |
| North Star | Poolster (de) | ['pōlstər] |
| Martian | marsmannetje (het) | ['mars·'manɛtʃə] |
| extraterrestrial (n) | buitenaards wezen (het) | ['bœʏtən·ārts 'wezən] |

| alien | bovenaards (het) | ['bɔvən·ārts] |
| flying saucer | vliegende schotel (de) | ['vlixəndə 'sxɔtəl] |
| | | |
| spaceship | ruimtevaartuig (het) | ['rœymtə·'vārtœyx] |
| space station | ruimtestation (het) | ['rœymtə·sta'tsjɔn] |
| blast-off | start (de) | [start] |
| | | |
| engine | motor (de) | ['mɔtɔr] |
| nozzle | straalpijp (de) | ['strāl·pɛjp] |
| fuel | brandstof (de) | ['brandstɔf] |
| | | |
| cockpit, flight deck | cabine (de) | [ka'binə] |
| antenna | antenne (de) | [an'tɛnə] |
| porthole | patrijspoort (de) | [pa'trɛjs·pōrt] |
| solar panel | zonnebatterij (de) | ['zɔnə·batə'rɛj] |
| spacesuit | ruimtepak (het) | ['rœymtə·pak] |
| | | |
| weightlessness | gewichtloosheid (de) | [xə'wixtlō'shɛjt] |
| oxygen | zuurstof (de) | ['zūrstɔf] |
| | | |
| docking (in space) | koppeling (de) | ['kɔpəliŋ] |
| to dock (vi, vt) | koppeling maken | ['kɔpəliŋ 'makən] |
| | | |
| observatory | observatorium (het) | [ɔbsɛrva'tɔrijum] |
| telescope | telescoop (de) | [telə'skōp] |
| to observe (vt) | waarnemen | ['wārnemən] |
| to explore (vt) | exploreren | [ɛksplɔ'rerən] |

## 75. The Earth

| the Earth | Aarde (de) | ['ārdə] |
| the globe (the Earth) | aardbol (de) | ['ārd·bɔl] |
| planet | planeet (de) | [pla'nēt] |
| | | |
| atmosphere | atmosfeer (de) | [atmɔ'sfēr] |
| geography | aardrijkskunde (de) | ['ārdrɛjkskʉndə] |
| nature | natuur (de) | [na'tūr] |
| | | |
| globe (table ~) | wereldbol (de) | ['werəld·bɔl] |
| map | kaart (de) | [kārt] |
| atlas | atlas (de) | ['atlas] |
| | | |
| Europe | Europa (het) | [ø'rɔpa] |
| Asia | Azië (het) | ['āzijə] |
| Africa | Afrika (het) | ['afrika] |
| Australia | Australië (het) | [ɔu'stralijə] |
| | | |
| America | Amerika (het) | [a'merika] |
| North America | Noord-Amerika (het) | [nōrd-a'merika] |
| South America | Zuid-Amerika (het) | ['zœyd-a'merika] |

| Antarctica | Antarctica (het) | [an'tarktika] |
| the Arctic | Arctis (de) | ['arktis] |

## 76. Cardinal directions

| north | noorden (het) | ['nõrdən] |
| to the north | naar het noorden | [nãr ət 'nõrdən] |
| in the north | in het noorden | [in ət 'nõrdən] |
| northern (adj) | noordelijk | ['nõrdələk] |

| south | zuiden (het) | ['zœʏdən] |
| to the south | naar het zuiden | [nãr ət zœʏdən] |
| in the south | in het zuiden | [in ət 'zœʏdən] |
| southern (adj) | zuidelijk | ['zœʏdələk] |

| west | westen (het) | ['wɛstən] |
| to the west | naar het westen | [nãr ət 'wɛstən] |
| in the west | in het westen | [in ət 'wɛstən] |
| western (adj) | westelijk | ['wɛstələk] |

| east | oosten (het) | ['õstən] |
| to the east | naar het oosten | [nãr ət 'õstən] |
| in the east | in het oosten | [in ət 'õstən] |
| eastern (adj) | oostelijk | ['õstələk] |

## 77. Sea. Ocean

| sea | zee (de) | [zẽ] |
| ocean | oceaan (de) | [ɔse'ãn] |
| gulf (bay) | golf (de) | [xɔlf] |
| straits | straat (de) | [strãt] |

| land (solid ground) | grond (de) | ['xrɔnt] |
| continent (mainland) | continent (het) | [kɔnti'nɛnt] |
| island | eiland (het) | ['ɛjlant] |
| peninsula | schiereiland (het) | ['sxir·ɛjlant] |
| archipelago | archipel (de) | [arxipɛl] |

| bay, cove | baai, bocht (de) | [bãj], [bɔxt] |
| harbor | haven (de) | ['havən] |
| lagoon | lagune (de) | [la'xʉnə] |
| cape | kaap (de) | [kãp] |

| atoll | atol (de) | [a'tɔl] |
| reef | rif (het) | [rif] |
| coral | koraal (het) | [kɔ'rãl] |
| coral reef | koraalrif (het) | [kɔ'rãl·rif] |
| deep (adj) | diep | [dip] |

| depth (deep water) | diepte (de) | ['diptə] |
| abyss | diepzee (de) | [dip·zē] |
| trench (e.g., Mariana ~) | trog (de) | [trɔx] |
| | | |
| current (Ocean ~) | stroming (de) | ['strɔmiŋ] |
| to surround (bathe) | omspoelen | ['ɔmspulən] |
| | | |
| shore | oever (de) | ['uvər] |
| coast | kust (de) | [kʊst] |
| | | |
| flow (flood tide) | vloed (de) | ['vlut] |
| ebb (ebb tide) | eb (de) | [ɛb] |
| shoal | ondiepte (de) | [ɔn'diptə] |
| bottom (~ of the sea) | bodem (de) | ['bɔdəm] |
| | | |
| wave | golf (de) | [xɔlf] |
| crest (~ of a wave) | golfkam (de) | ['xɔlfkam] |
| spume (sea foam) | schuim (het) | ['sxœʏm] |
| | | |
| storm (sea storm) | storm (de) | [stɔrm] |
| hurricane | orkaan (de) | [ɔr'kān] |
| tsunami | tsunami (de) | [tsu'nami] |
| calm (dead ~) | windstilte (de) | ['wind·stiltə] |
| quiet, calm (adj) | kalm | [kalm] |
| | | |
| pole | pool (de) | [pōl] |
| polar (adj) | polair | [pɔ'lɛr] |
| | | |
| latitude | breedtegraad (de) | ['brētə·xrāt] |
| longitude | lengtegraad (de) | ['lɛŋtə·xrāt] |
| parallel | parallel (de) | [para'lɛl] |
| equator | evenaar (de) | ['ɛvənār] |
| | | |
| sky | hemel (de) | ['heməl] |
| horizon | horizon (de) | ['hɔrizɔn] |
| air | lucht (de) | [lʊxt] |
| | | |
| lighthouse | vuurtoren (de) | ['vūr·tɔrən] |
| to dive (vi) | duiken | ['dœʏkən] |
| to sink (ab. boat) | zinken | ['zinkən] |
| treasures | schatten | ['sxatən] |

## 78. Seas' and Oceans' names

| Atlantic Ocean | Atlantische Oceaan (de) | [at'lantisə ɔse'ān] |
| Indian Ocean | Indische Oceaan (de) | ['indisə ɔse'ān] |
| Pacific Ocean | Stille Oceaan (de) | ['stilə ɔse'ān] |
| Arctic Ocean | Noordelijke IJszee (de) | ['nōrdələkə 'ɛjs·zē] |
| Black Sea | Zwarte Zee (de) | ['zwartə zē] |
| Red Sea | Rode Zee (de) | ['rɔdə zē] |

| Yellow Sea | Gele Zee (de) | ['xelə zē] |
| White Sea | Witte Zee (de) | ['witə zē] |

| Caspian Sea | Kaspische Zee (de) | ['kaspisə zē] |
| Dead Sea | Dode Zee (de) | ['dɔdə zē] |
| Mediterranean Sea | Middellandse Zee (de) | ['midəlandsə zē] |

| Aegean Sea | Egeïsche Zee (de) | [ɛ'xejsə zē] |
| Adriatic Sea | Adriatische Zee (de) | [adri'atisə zē] |

| Arabian Sea | Arabische Zee (de) | [a'rabisə zē] |
| Sea of Japan | Japanse Zee (de) | [ja'pansə zē] |
| Bering Sea | Beringzee (de) | ['beriŋ·zē] |
| South China Sea | Zuid-Chinese Zee (de) | ['zœyd-ʃi'nesə zē] |

| Coral Sea | Koraalzee (de) | [kɔ'rāl·zē] |
| Tasman Sea | Tasmanzee (de) | ['tasman·zē] |
| Caribbean Sea | Caribische Zee (de) | [ka'ribisə zē] |

| Barents Sea | Barentszzee (de) | ['barənts·zē] |
| Kara Sea | Karische Zee (de) | ['karisə zē] |

| North Sea | Noordzee (de) | ['nōrd·zē] |
| Baltic Sea | Baltische Zee (de) | ['baltisə zē] |
| Norwegian Sea | Noorse Zee (de) | ['nōrsə zē] |

## 79. Mountains

| mountain | berg (de) | [bɛrx] |
| mountain range | bergketen (de) | ['bɛrx·'ketən] |
| mountain ridge | gebergte (het) | [xə'bɛrxtə] |

| summit, top | bergtop (de) | ['bɛrx·tɔp] |
| peak | bergpiek (de) | ['bɛrx·pik] |
| foot (~ of the mountain) | voet (de) | [vut] |
| slope (mountainside) | helling (de) | ['heliŋ] |

| volcano | vulkaan (de) | [vʉl'kān] |
| active volcano | actieve vulkaan (de) | [ak'tivə vʉl'kān] |
| dormant volcano | uitgedoofde vulkaan (de) | ['œytxədōfdə vyl'kān] |

| eruption | uitbarsting (de) | ['œytbarstiŋ] |
| crater | krater (de) | ['kratər] |
| magma | magma (het) | ['maxma] |
| lava | lava (de) | ['lava] |
| molten (~ lava) | gloeiend | ['xlʉjənt] |

| canyon | kloof (de) | [klōf] |
| gorge | bergkloof (de) | ['bɛrx·klōf] |
| crevice | spleet (de) | [splet] |

| | | |
|---|---|---|
| abyss (chasm) | **afgrond (de)** | ['afxrɔnt] |
| pass, col | **bergpas (de)** | ['bɛrx·pas] |
| plateau | **plateau (het)** | [pla'tɔ] |
| cliff | **klip (de)** | [klip] |
| hill | **heuvel (de)** | ['høvəl] |
| | | |
| glacier | **gletsjer (de)** | ['xletʃər] |
| waterfall | **waterval (de)** | ['watər·val] |
| geyser | **geiser (de)** | ['xɛjzər] |
| lake | **meer (het)** | [mēr] |
| | | |
| plain | **vlakte (de)** | ['vlaktə] |
| landscape | **landschap (het)** | ['landsxap] |
| echo | **echo (de)** | ['ɛxɔ] |
| | | |
| alpinist | **alpinist (de)** | [alpi'nist] |
| rock climber | **bergbeklimmer (de)** | ['bɛrx·bə'klimər] |
| to conquer (in climbing) | **trotseren** | [trɔ'tserən] |
| climb (an easy ~) | **beklimming (de)** | [bə'klimiŋ] |

## 80. Mountains names

| | | |
|---|---|---|
| The Alps | **Alpen (de)** | ['alpən] |
| Mont Blanc | **Mont Blanc (de)** | [mɔn blan] |
| The Pyrenees | **Pyreneeën (de)** | [pirə'nēən] |
| | | |
| The Carpathians | **Karpaten (de)** | [kar'patən] |
| The Ural Mountains | **Oeralgebergte (het)** | [ural·xə'bɛrxtə] |
| The Caucasus Mountains | **Kaukasus (de)** | [kau'kazʉs] |
| Mount Elbrus | **Elbroes (de)** | [ɛlb'rus] |
| | | |
| The Altai Mountains | **Altaj (de)** | [al'taj] |
| The Tian Shan | **Tiensjan (de)** | [ti'enɕan] |
| The Pamir Mountains | **Pamir (de)** | [pa'mir] |
| The Himalayas | **Himalaya (de)** | [hima'laja] |
| Mount Everest | **Everest (de)** | ['ɛverɛst] |
| | | |
| The Andes | **Andes (de)** | ['andɛs] |
| Mount Kilimanjaro | **Kilimanjaro (de)** | [kiliman'dʒarɔ] |

## 81. Rivers

| | | |
|---|---|---|
| river | **rivier (de)** | [ri'vir] |
| spring (natural source) | **bron (de)** | [brɔn] |
| riverbed (river channel) | **rivierbedding (de)** | [ri'vir·'bɛdiŋ] |
| basin (river valley) | **rivierbekken (het)** | [ri'vir·'bɛkən] |
| to flow into … | **uitmonden in …** | ['œʏtmɔndən in] |
| tributary | **zijrivier (de)** | [zɛj·ri'vir] |

| | | |
|---|---|---|
| bank (of river) | oever (de) | ['uvər] |
| current (stream) | stroming (de) | ['strɔmiŋ] |
| downstream (adv) | stroomafwaarts | [strōm·'afwārts] |
| upstream (adv) | stroomopwaarts | [strōm·'ɔpwārts] |
| inundation | overstroming (de) | [ɔvər'strɔmiŋ] |
| flooding | overstroming (de) | [ɔvər'strɔmiŋ] |
| to overflow (vi) | buiten zijn | ['bœytən zɛjn |
| | oevers treden | 'uvərs 'trɛdən] |
| to flood (vt) | overstromen | [ɔvər'strɔmən] |
| shallow (shoal) | zandbank (de) | ['zant·bank] |
| rapids | stroomversnelling (de) | [strōm·vər'sneliŋ] |
| dam | dam (de) | [dam] |
| canal | kanaal (het) | [ka'nāl] |
| reservoir (artificial lake) | spaarbekken (het) | ['spār·bɛkən] |
| sluice, lock | sluis (de) | ['slœys] |
| water body (pond, etc.) | waterlichaam (het) | ['watər·'lixām] |
| swamp (marshland) | moeras (het) | [mu'ras] |
| bog, marsh | broek (het) | [bruk] |
| whirlpool | draaikolk (de) | ['drāj·kɔlk] |
| stream (brook) | stroom (de) | [strōm] |
| drinking (ab. water) | drink- | [drink] |
| fresh (~ water) | zoet | [zut] |
| ice | ijs (het) | [ɛjs] |
| to freeze over | bevriezen | [bə'vrizən] |
| (ab. river, etc.) | | |

## 82. Rivers' names

| | | |
|---|---|---|
| Seine | Seine (de) | ['sɛjnə] |
| Loire | Loire (de) | [lu'arə] |
| Thames | Theems (de) | ['tɛjms] |
| Rhine | Rijn (de) | ['rɛjn] |
| Danube | Donau (de) | ['dɔnau] |
| Volga | Wolga (de) | ['wɔlxa] |
| Don | Don (de) | [dɔn] |
| Lena | Lena (de) | ['lena] |
| Yellow River | Gele Rivier (de) | ['xelə ri'vir] |
| Yangtze | Blauwe Rivier (de) | ['blauə ri'vir] |
| Mekong | Mekong (de) | [me'kɔŋ] |
| Ganges | Ganges (de) | ['xaŋəs] |
| Nile River | Nijl (de) | ['nɛjl] |

| Congo River | **Kongo (de)** | [ˈkɔnxɔ] |
| Okavango River | **Okavango (de)** | [ɔkaˈvanxɔ] |
| Zambezi River | **Zambezi (de)** | [zamˈbezi] |
| Limpopo River | **Limpopo (de)** | [limˈpɔpɔ] |
| Mississippi River | **Mississippi (de)** | [misiˈsipi] |

## 83. Forest

| forest, wood | **bos (het)** | [bɔs] |
| forest (as adj) | **bos-** | [bɔs] |
| | | |
| thick forest | **oerwoud (het)** | [ˈurwaut] |
| grove | **bosje (het)** | [ˈbɔɕə] |
| forest clearing | **open plek (de)** | [ˈɔpən plek] |
| | | |
| thicket | **struikgewas (het)** | [ˈstrœɥk·xəˈwas] |
| scrubland | **struiken** | [ˈstrœɥkən] |
| | | |
| footpath (troddenpath) | **paadje (het)** | [ˈpādjə] |
| gully | **ravijn (het)** | [raˈvɛjn] |
| | | |
| tree | **boom (de)** | [bōm] |
| leaf | **blad (het)** | [blat] |
| leaves (foliage) | **gebladerte (het)** | [xəˈbladərtə] |
| | | |
| fall of leaves | **vallende bladeren** | [ˈvaləndə ˈbladerən] |
| to fall (ab. leaves) | **vallen** | [ˈvalən] |
| top (of the tree) | **boomtop (de)** | [ˈbōm·tɔp] |
| | | |
| branch | **tak (de)** | [tak] |
| bough | **ent (de)** | [ɛnt] |
| bud (on shrub, tree) | **knop (de)** | [knɔp] |
| needle (of pine tree) | **naald (de)** | [nālt] |
| pine cone | **dennenappel (de)** | [ˈdɛnən·ˈapəl] |
| | | |
| hollow (in a tree) | **boom holte (de)** | [bōm ˈhɔltə] |
| nest | **nest (het)** | [nɛst] |
| burrow (animal hole) | **hol (het)** | [hɔl] |
| | | |
| trunk | **stam (de)** | [stam] |
| root | **wortel (de)** | [ˈwɔrtəl] |
| bark | **schors (de)** | [sxɔrs] |
| moss | **mos (het)** | [mɔs] |
| | | |
| to uproot (remove trees or tree stumps) | **ontwortelen** | [ɔntˈwɔrtələn] |
| to chop down | **kappen** | [ˈkapən] |
| to deforest (vt) | **ontbossen** | [ɔnˈbɔsən] |
| tree stump | **stronk (de)** | [strɔnk] |
| campfire | **kampvuur (het)** | [ˈkampvūr] |

| forest fire | bosbrand (de) | ['bɔs·brant] |
| to extinguish (vt) | blussen | ['blʉsən] |

| forest ranger | boswachter (de) | [bɔs·'waxtər] |
| protection | bescherming (de) | [bə'sxɛrmiŋ] |
| to protect (~ nature) | beschermen | [bə'sxɛrmən] |
| poacher | stroper (de) | ['strɔpər] |
| steel trap | val (de) | [val] |

| to gather, to pick (vt) | plukken | ['plʉkən] |
| to lose one's way | verdwalen | [vərd'walən] |
| | (de weg kwijt zijn) | |

## 84. Natural resources

| natural resources | natuurlijke rijkdommen | [na'tʉrləkə 'rɛjkdɔmən] |
| minerals | delfstoffen | ['dɛlfstɔfən] |
| deposits | lagen | ['laxən] |
| field (e.g., oilfield) | veld (het) | [vɛlt] |

| to mine (extract) | winnen | ['winən] |
| mining (extraction) | winning (de) | ['winiŋ] |
| ore | erts (het) | [ɛrts] |
| mine (e.g., for coal) | mijn (de) | [mɛjn] |
| shaft (mine ~) | mijnschacht (de) | ['mɛjn·sxaxt] |
| miner | mijnwerker (de) | ['mɛjn·wɛrkər] |

| gas (natural ~) | gas (het) | [xas] |
| gas pipeline | gasleiding (de) | [xas·'lɛjdiŋ] |

| oil (petroleum) | olie (de) | ['ɔli] |
| oil pipeline | olieleiding (de) | ['ɔli·'lɛjdiŋ] |
| oil well | oliebron (de) | ['ɔli·brɔn] |
| derrick (tower) | boortoren (de) | [bōr·'tɔrən] |
| tanker | tanker (de) | ['tankər] |

| sand | zand (het) | [zant] |
| limestone | kalksteen (de) | ['kalkstēn] |
| gravel | grind (het) | [xrint] |
| peat | veen (het) | [vēn] |
| clay | klei (de) | [klɛj] |
| coal | steenkool (de) | ['stēn·kōl] |

| iron (ore) | ijzer (het) | ['ɛjzər] |
| gold | goud (het) | ['xaut] |
| silver | zilver (het) | ['zilvər] |
| nickel | nikkel (het) | ['nikəl] |
| copper | koper (het) | ['kopər] |
| zinc | zink (het) | [zink] |
| manganese | mangaan (het) | [man'xān] |

| mercury | kwik (het) | ['kwik] |
| lead | lood (het) | [lõt] |

| mineral | mineraal (het) | [minə'rāl] |
| crystal | kristal (het) | [kris'tal] |
| marble | marmer (het) | ['marmər] |
| uranium | uraan (het) | [ju'rān] |

## 85. Weather

| weather | weer (het) | [wẽr] |
| weather forecast | weersvoorspelling (de) | ['wẽrs·vōr'spɛliŋ] |
| temperature | temperatuur (de) | [tɛmpəra'tūr] |
| thermometer | thermometer (de) | ['tɛrmɔmetər] |
| barometer | barometer (de) | ['barɔ'metər] |

| humid (adj) | vochtig | ['vɔhtəx] |
| humidity | vochtigheid (de) | ['vɔhtixhɛjt] |
| heat (extreme ~) | hitte (de) | ['hitə] |
| hot (torrid) | heet | [hẽt] |
| it's hot | het is heet | [ət is hẽt] |

| it's warm | het is warm | [ət is warm] |
| warm (moderately hot) | warm | [warm] |

| it's cold | het is koud | [ət is 'kaut] |
| cold (adj) | koud | ['kaut] |

| sun | zon (de) | [zɔn] |
| to shine (vi) | schijnen | ['sxɛjnən] |
| sunny (day) | zonnig | ['zɔnɛx] |
| to come up (vi) | opgaan | ['ɔpxān] |
| to set (vi) | ondergaan | ['ɔndərxān] |

| cloud | wolk (de) | [wɔlk] |
| cloudy (adj) | bewolkt | [bə'wɔlkt] |
| rain cloud | regenwolk (de) | ['rexən·wɔlk] |
| somber (gloomy) | somber | ['sɔmbər] |

| rain | regen (de) | ['rexən] |
| it's raining | het regent | [ət 'rexənt] |
| rainy (~ day, weather) | regenachtig | ['rexənaxtəx] |
| to drizzle (vi) | motregenen | ['mɔtrexənən] |

| pouring rain | plensbui (de) | ['plɛnsbœɣ] |
| downpour | stortbui (de) | ['stɔrt·bœɣ] |
| heavy (e.g., ~ rain) | hard | [hart] |
| puddle | plas (de) | [plas] |
| to get wet (in rain) | nat worden | [nat 'wɔrdən] |
| fog (mist) | mist (de) | [mist] |

| foggy | mistig | ['mistəx] |
| snow | sneeuw (de) | [snēw] |
| it's snowing | het sneeuwt | [ət 'snēwt] |

## 86. Severe weather. Natural disasters

| thunderstorm | noodweer (het) | ['nɔtwer] |
| lightning (~ strike) | bliksem (de) | ['bliksəm] |
| to flash (vi) | flitsen | ['flitsən] |

| thunder | donder (de) | ['dɔndər] |
| to thunder (vi) | donderen | ['dɔndərən] |
| it's thundering | het dondert | [ət 'dɔndərt] |

| hail | hagel (de) | ['haxəl] |
| it's hailing | het hagelt | [ət 'haxəlt] |

| to flood (vt) | overstromen | [ɔvər'strɔmən] |
| flood, inundation | overstroming (de) | [ɔvər'strɔmiŋ] |

| earthquake | aardbeving (de) | ['ārd·beviŋ] |
| tremor, quake | aardschok (de) | ['ārd·sxɔk] |
| epicenter | epicentrum (het) | [ɛpi'sɛntrʉm] |

| eruption | uitbarsting (de) | ['œytbarstiŋ] |
| lava | lava (de) | ['lava] |

| twister | wervelwind (de) | ['wɛrvəl·vint] |
| tornado | windhoos (de) | ['windhōs] |
| typhoon | tyfoon (de) | [taj'fōn] |

| hurricane | orkaan (de) | [ɔr'kān] |
| storm | storm (de) | [stɔrm] |
| tsunami | tsunami (de) | [tsʉ'nami] |

| cyclone | cycloon (de) | [si'klōn] |
| bad weather | onweer (het) | ['ɔnwēr] |
| fire (accident) | brand (de) | [brant] |
| disaster | ramp (de) | [ramp] |
| meteorite | meteoriet (de) | [meteɔ'rit] |

| avalanche | lawine (de) | [la'winə] |
| snowslide | sneeuwverschuiving (de) | ['snēw·'fɛrsxœyviŋ] |
| blizzard | sneeuwjacht (de) | ['snēw·jaxt] |
| snowstorm | sneeuwstorm (de) | ['snēw·stɔrm] |

T&P BOOKS

# FAUNA

T&P Books Publishing

## 87. Mammals. Predators

| | | |
|---|---|---|
| predator | roofdier (het) | ['rōf·dīr] |
| tiger | tijger (de) | ['tɛjxər] |
| lion | leeuw (de) | [lēw] |
| wolf | wolf (de) | [wɔlf] |
| fox | vos (de) | [vɔs] |
| jaguar | jaguar (de) | ['jaguar] |
| leopard | luipaard (de) | ['lœʏpārt] |
| cheetah | jachtluipaard (de) | ['jaxt·lœʏpārt] |
| black panther | panter (de) | ['pantər] |
| puma | poema (de) | ['puma] |
| snow leopard | sneeuwluipaard (de) | ['snēw·lœʏpārt] |
| lynx | lynx (de) | [links] |
| coyote | coyote (de) | [kɔ'jot] |
| jackal | jakhals (de) | ['jakhals] |
| hyena | hyena (de) | [hi'ena] |

## 88. Wild animals

| | | |
|---|---|---|
| animal | dier (het) | [dīr] |
| beast (animal) | beest (het) | [bēst] |
| squirrel | eekhoorn (de) | ['ēkhōrn] |
| hedgehog | egel (de) | ['exəl] |
| hare | haas (de) | [hās] |
| rabbit | konijn (het) | [kɔ'nɛjn] |
| badger | das (de) | [das] |
| raccoon | wasbeer (de) | ['wasbēr] |
| hamster | hamster (de) | ['hamstər] |
| marmot | marmot (de) | [mar'mɔt] |
| mole | mol (de) | [mɔl] |
| mouse | muis (de) | [mœʏs] |
| rat | rat (de) | [rat] |
| bat | vleermuis (de) | ['vlēr·mœʏs] |
| ermine | hermelijn (de) | [hɛrmə'lɛjn] |
| sable | sabeldier (het) | ['sabəl·dīr] |
| marten | marter (de) | ['martər] |

| weasel | **wezel (de)** | ['wezəl] |
| mink | **nerts (de)** | [nɛrts] |

| beaver | **bever (de)** | ['bɛvər] |
| otter | **otter (de)** | ['ɔtər] |

| horse | **paard (het)** | [pārt] |
| moose | **eland (de)** | ['ɛlant] |
| deer | **hert (het)** | [hɛrt] |
| camel | **kameel (de)** | [ka'mēl] |

| bison | **bizon (de)** | [bi'zɔn] |
| aurochs | **oeros (de)** | ['urɔs] |
| buffalo | **buffel (de)** | ['bʉfəl] |

| zebra | **zebra (de)** | ['zɛbra] |
| antelope | **antilope (de)** | [anti'lɔpə] |
| roe deer | **ree (de)** | [rē] |
| fallow deer | **damhert (het)** | ['damhɛrt] |
| chamois | **gems (de)** | [xɛms] |
| wild boar | **everzwijn (het)** | ['ɛvər·zwɛjn] |

| whale | **walvis (de)** | ['walvis] |
| seal | **rob (de)** | [rɔb] |
| walrus | **walrus (de)** | ['walrʉs] |
| fur seal | **zeehond (de)** | ['zē·hɔnt] |
| dolphin | **dolfijn (de)** | [dɔl'fɛjn] |

| bear | **beer (de)** | [bēr] |
| polar bear | **ijsbeer (de)** | ['ɛjs·bēr] |
| panda | **panda (de)** | ['panda] |

| monkey | **aap (de)** | [āp] |
| chimpanzee | **chimpansee (de)** | [ʃimpan'sē] |
| orangutan | **orang-oetan (de)** | [ɔ'raŋ-utaŋ] |
| gorilla | **gorilla (de)** | [xɔ'rila] |
| macaque | **makaak (de)** | [ma'kāk] |
| gibbon | **gibbon (de)** | ['xibɔn] |

| elephant | **olifant (de)** | ['ɔlifant] |
| rhinoceros | **neushoorn (de)** | ['nøshōrn] |

| giraffe | **giraffe (de)** | [xi'rafə] |
| hippopotamus | **nijlpaard (het)** | ['nɛjl·pārt] |

| kangaroo | **kangoeroe (de)** | ['kanxəru] |
| koala (bear) | **koala (de)** | [kɔ'ala] |

| mongoose | **mangoest (de)** | [man'xust] |
| chinchilla | **chinchilla (de)** | [ʃin'ʃila] |
| skunk | **stinkdier (het)** | ['stiɳk·dīr] |
| porcupine | **stekelvarken (het)** | ['stekəl·'varkən] |

## 89. Domestic animals

| cat | poes (de) | [pus] |
| tomcat | kater (de) | ['katər] |

| horse | paard (het) | [pãrt] |
| stallion (male horse) | hengst (de) | [hɛŋst] |
| mare | merrie (de) | ['mɛri] |

| cow | koe (de) | [ku] |
| bull | stier (de) | [stir] |
| ox | os (de) | [ɔs] |

| sheep (ewe) | schaap (het) | [sxãp] |
| ram | ram (de) | [ram] |
| goat | geit (de) | [xɛjt] |
| billy goat, he-goat | bok (de) | [bɔk] |

| donkey | ezel (de) | ['ezəl] |
| mule | muilezel (de) | [mœylezəl] |

| pig, hog | varken (het) | ['varkən] |
| piglet | biggetje (het) | ['bixətʃə] |
| rabbit | konijn (het) | [kɔ'nɛjn] |

| hen (chicken) | kip (de) | [kip] |
| rooster | haan (de) | [hãn] |

| duck | eend (de) | [ēnt] |
| drake | woerd (de) | [wurt] |
| goose | gans (de) | [xans] |

| tom turkey, gobbler | kalkoen haan (de) | [kal'kun hãn] |
| turkey (hen) | kalkoen (de) | [kal'kun] |

| domestic animals | huisdieren | ['hœys·'dīrən] |
| tame (e.g., ~ hamster) | tam | [tam] |
| to tame (vt) | temmen, tam maken | ['tɛmən], [tam 'makən] |
| to breed (vt) | fokken | ['fɔkən] |

| farm | boerderij (de) | [burdə'rɛj] |
| poultry | gevogelte (het) | [xə'vɔxəltə] |

| cattle | rundvee (het) | ['rʉntvē] |
| herd (cattle) | kudde (de) | ['kʉdə] |

| stable | paardenstal (de) | ['pãrdən·stal] |
| pigpen | zwijnenstal (de) | ['zwɛjnən·stal] |
| cowshed | koeienstal (de) | ['kujen·stal] |
| rabbit hutch | konijnenhok (het) | [kɔ'nɛjnən·hɔk] |
| hen house | kippenhok (het) | ['kipən·hɔk] |

## 90. Birds

| bird | vogel (de) | ['vɔxəl] |
| pigeon | duif (de) | ['dœyf] |
| sparrow | mus (de) | [mʉs] |
| tit (great tit) | koolmees (de) | ['kōlmēs] |
| magpie | ekster (de) | ['ɛkstər] |

| raven | raaf (de) | [rāf] |
| crow | kraai (de) | [krāj] |
| jackdaw | kauw (de) | ['kau] |
| rook | roek (de) | [ruk] |

| duck | eend (de) | [ēnt] |
| goose | gans (de) | [xans] |
| pheasant | fazant (de) | [fa'zant] |

| eagle | arend (de) | ['arənt] |
| hawk | havik (de) | ['havik] |
| falcon | valk (de) | [valk] |
| vulture | gier (de) | [xir] |
| condor (Andean ~) | condor (de) | ['kɔndɔr] |

| swan | zwaan (de) | [zwān] |
| crane | kraanvogel (de) | ['krān·vɔxəl] |
| stork | ooievaar (de) | ['ōjevār] |

| parrot | papegaai (de) | [papə'xāj] |
| hummingbird | kolibrie (de) | [kɔ'libri] |
| peacock | pauw (de) | ['pau] |

| ostrich | struisvogel (de) | ['strœys·vɔxəl] |
| heron | reiger (de) | ['rɛjxər] |
| flamingo | flamingo (de) | [fla'mingɔ] |
| pelican | pelikaan (de) | [peli'kān] |

| nightingale | nachtegaal (de) | ['nahtəxāl] |
| swallow | zwaluw (de) | ['zwalʉv] |

| thrush | lijster (de) | ['lɛjstər] |
| song thrush | zanglijster (de) | [zaŋ·'lɛjstər] |
| blackbird | merel (de) | ['merəl] |

| swift | gierzwaluw (de) | [xirz'walʉw] |
| lark | leeuwerik (de) | ['lēwərik] |
| quail | kwartel (de) | ['kwartəl] |

| woodpecker | specht (de) | [spɛxt] |
| cuckoo | koekoek (de) | ['kukuk] |
| owl | uil (de) | ['œyl] |
| eagle owl | oehoe (de) | ['uhu] |

| wood grouse | auerhoen (het) | ['auər·hun] |
| black grouse | korhoen (het) | ['kɔrhun] |
| partridge | patrijs (de) | [pa'trɛjs] |

| starling | spreeuw (de) | [sprēw] |
| canary | kanarie (de) | [ka'nari] |
| hazel grouse | hazelhoen (het) | ['hazəlhun] |
| chaffinch | vink (de) | [vink] |
| bullfinch | goudvink (de) | ['xaudvink] |

| seagull | meeuw (de) | [mēw] |
| albatross | albatros (de) | [albatrɔs] |
| penguin | pinguïn (de) | ['piŋgwin] |

## 91. Fish. Marine animals

| bream | brasem (de) | ['brasəm] |
| carp | karper (de) | ['karpər] |
| perch | baars (de) | [bārs] |
| catfish | meerval (de) | ['mērval] |
| pike | snoek (de) | [snuk] |

| salmon | zalm (de) | [zalm] |
| sturgeon | steur (de) | ['stør] |

| herring | haring (de) | ['hariŋ] |
| Atlantic salmon | atlantische zalm (de) | [at'lantisə zalm] |
| mackerel | makreel (de) | [ma'krēl] |
| flatfish | platvis (de) | ['platvis] |

| zander, pike perch | snoekbaars (de) | ['snukbārs] |
| cod | kabeljauw (de) | [kabə'ljau] |
| tuna | tonijn (de) | [tɔ'nɛjn] |
| trout | forel (de) | [fɔ'rɛl] |

| eel | paling (de) | [pa'liŋ] |
| electric ray | sidderrog (de) | ['sidər·rɔx] |
| moray eel | murene (de) | [mʉ'rɛnə] |
| piranha | piranha (de) | [pi'ranja] |

| shark | haai (de) | [hāj] |
| dolphin | dolfijn (de) | [dɔl'fɛjn] |
| whale | walvis (de) | ['walvis] |

| crab | krab (de) | [krab] |
| jellyfish | kwal (de) | ['kwal] |
| octopus | octopus (de) | ['ɔktɔpʉs] |

| starfish | zeester (de) | ['zē·stər] |
| sea urchin | zee-egel (de) | [zē-'exəl] |

| seahorse | zeepaardje (het) | ['zē·pārtjə] |
| oyster | oester (de) | ['ustər] |
| shrimp | garnaal (de) | [xar'nāl] |
| lobster | kreeft (de) | [krēft] |
| spiny lobster | langoest (de) | [lan'xust] |

## 92. Amphibians. Reptiles

| snake | slang (de) | [slaŋ] |
| venomous (snake) | giftig | ['xiftəx] |
| | | |
| viper | adder (de) | ['adər] |
| cobra | cobra (de) | ['kɔbra] |
| python | python (de) | ['pitɔn] |
| boa | boa (de) | ['bɔa] |
| | | |
| grass snake | ringslang (de) | ['riŋ·slaŋ] |
| rattle snake | ratelslang (de) | ['ratəl·slaŋ] |
| anaconda | anaconda (de) | [ana'kɔnda] |
| | | |
| lizard | hagedis (de) | ['haxədis] |
| iguana | leguaan (de) | [lexʉ'ān] |
| monitor lizard | varaan (de) | [va'rān] |
| salamander | salamander (de) | [sala'mandər] |
| chameleon | kameleon (de) | [kamele'ɔn] |
| scorpion | schorpioen (de) | [sxɔrpi'un] |
| | | |
| turtle | schildpad (de) | ['sxildpat] |
| frog | kikker (de) | ['kikər] |
| toad | pad (de) | [pat] |
| crocodile | krokodil (de) | [krɔkɔ'dil] |

## 93. Insects

| insect, bug | insect (het) | [in'sɛkt] |
| butterfly | vlinder (de) | ['vlindər] |
| ant | mier (de) | [mir] |
| fly | vlieg (de) | [vlix] |
| mosquito | mug (de) | [mʉx] |
| beetle | kever (de) | ['kevər] |
| | | |
| wasp | wesp (de) | [wɛsp] |
| bee | bij (de) | [bɛj] |
| bumblebee | hommel (de) | ['hɔməl] |
| gadfly (botfly) | horzel (de) | ['hɔrsəl] |
| | | |
| spider | spin (de) | [spin] |
| spiderweb | spinnenweb (het) | ['spinən·wɛb] |

| | | |
|---|---|---|
| dragonfly | libel (de) | [li'bɛl] |
| grasshopper | sprinkhaan (de) | ['sprinkhān] |
| moth (night butterfly) | nachtvlinder (de) | ['naxt·'vlindər] |
| | | |
| cockroach | kakkerlak (de) | ['kakərlak] |
| tick | teek (de) | [tēk] |
| flea | vlo (de) | [vlɔ] |
| midge | kriebelmug (de) | ['kribəl·mʉx] |
| | | |
| locust | treksprinkhaan (de) | ['trɛk·sprink'hān] |
| snail | slak (de) | [slak] |
| cricket | krekel (de) | ['krekəl] |
| lightning bug | glimworm (de) | ['xlim·wɔrm] |
| ladybug | lieveheersbeestje (het) | [livə'hērs·'bestʃə] |
| cockchafer | meikever (de) | ['mɛjkəvər] |
| | | |
| leech | bloedzuiger (de) | ['blud·zœɣxər] |
| caterpillar | rups (de) | [rʉps] |
| earthworm | aardworm (de) | ['ārd·wɔrm] |
| larva | larve (de) | ['larvə] |

# FLORA

**T&P Books Publishing**

| tree | boom (de) | [bõm] |
|---|---|---|
| deciduous (adj) | loof- | [lõf] |
| coniferous (adj) | dennen- | ['dɛnən] |
| evergreen (adj) | groenblijvend | [xrun 'blɛjvənt] |

| apple tree | appelboom (de) | ['apəl·bõm] |
|---|---|---|
| pear tree | perenboom (de) | ['perən·bõm] |
| sweet cherry tree | zoete kers (de) | ['zutə kɛrs] |
| sour cherry tree | zure kers (de) | ['zʉrə kɛrs] |
| plum tree | pruimelaar (de) | [prœʏmə·lãr] |

| birch | berk (de) | [bɛrk] |
|---|---|---|
| oak | eik (de) | [ɛjk] |
| linden tree | linde (de) | ['lində] |
| aspen | esp (de) | [ɛsp] |
| maple | esdoorn (de) | ['ɛsdõrn] |

| spruce | spar (de) | [spar] |
|---|---|---|
| pine | den (de) | [dɛn] |
| larch | lariks (de) | ['lariks] |

| fir tree | zilverspar (de) | ['zilvər·spar] |
|---|---|---|
| cedar | ceder (de) | ['sedər] |

| poplar | populier (de) | [popʉ'lir] |
|---|---|---|
| rowan | lijsterbes (de) | ['lɛjstərbɛs] |

| willow | wilg (de) | [wilx] |
|---|---|---|
| alder | els (de) | [ɛls] |

| beech | beuk (de) | ['bøk] |
|---|---|---|
| elm | iep (de) | [jep] |

| ash (tree) | es (de) | [ɛs] |
|---|---|---|
| chestnut | kastanje (de) | [kas'tanjə] |

| magnolia | magnolia (de) | [mah'nɔlija] |
|---|---|---|
| palm tree | palm (de) | [palm] |
| cypress | cipres (de) | [sip'rɛs] |

| mangrove | mangrove (de) | [man'xrɔvə] |
|---|---|---|
| baobab | baobab (de) | ['baɔbap] |
| eucalyptus | eucalyptus (de) | [øka'liptʉs] |
| sequoia | mammoetboom (de) | [ma'mut·bõm] |

## 95. Shrubs

| | | |
|---|---|---|
| bush | struik (de) | ['strœʏk] |
| shrub | heester (de) | ['hēstər] |
| | | |
| grapevine | wijnstok (de) | ['wɛjn·stɔk] |
| vineyard | wijngaard (de) | ['wɛjnxārt] |
| | | |
| raspberry bush | frambozenstruik (de) | [fram'bɔsən·'strœʏk] |
| blackcurrant bush | zwarte bes (de) | ['zwartə bɛs] |
| redcurrant bush | rode bessenstruik (de) | ['rɔdə 'bɛsən·strœʏk] |
| gooseberry bush | kruisbessenstruik (de) | ['krœʏs·'bɛsənstrœʏk] |
| | | |
| acacia | acacia (de) | [a'kaɕia] |
| barberry | zuurbes (de) | ['zūr·bɛs] |
| jasmine | jasmijn (de) | [jas'mɛjn] |
| | | |
| juniper | jeneverbes (de) | [je'nɛvərbɛs] |
| rosebush | rozenstruik (de) | ['rɔzən·strœʏk] |
| dog rose | hondsroos (de) | ['hund·rōs] |

## 96. Fruits. Berries

| | | |
|---|---|---|
| fruit | vrucht (de) | [vrʉxt] |
| fruits | vruchten | ['vrʉxtən] |
| apple | appel (de) | ['apəl] |
| pear | peer (de) | [pēr] |
| plum | pruim (de) | ['prœʏm] |
| | | |
| strawberry (garden ~) | aardbei (de) | ['ārd·bɛj] |
| sour cherry | zure kers (de) | ['zʉrə kɛrs] |
| sweet cherry | zoete kers (de) | ['zutə kɛrs] |
| grape | druif (de) | [drœʏf] |
| | | |
| raspberry | framboos (de) | [fram'bōs] |
| blackcurrant | zwarte bes (de) | ['zwartə bɛs] |
| redcurrant | rode bes (de) | ['rɔdə bɛs] |
| gooseberry | kruisbes (de) | ['krœʏsbɛs] |
| cranberry | veenbes (de) | ['vēnbɛs] |
| | | |
| orange | sinaasappel (de) | ['sināsapəl] |
| mandarin | mandarijn (de) | [manda'rɛjn] |
| pineapple | ananas (de) | ['ananas] |
| banana | banaan (de) | [ba'nān] |
| date | dadel (de) | ['dadəl] |
| | | |
| lemon | citroen (de) | [si'trun] |
| apricot | abrikoos (de) | [abri'kōs] |
| peach | perzik (de) | ['pɛrzik] |

| kiwi | kiwi (de) | ['kiwi] |
| grapefruit | grapefruit (de) | ['grepfrut] |

| berry | bes (de) | [bɛs] |
| berries | bessen | ['bɛsən] |
| cowberry | vossenbes (de) | ['vɔsənbɛs] |
| wild strawberry | bosaardbei (de) | [bɔs·ārdbɛj] |
| bilberry | bosbes (de) | ['bɔsbɛs] |

## 97. Flowers. Plants

| flower | bloem (de) | [blum] |
| bouquet (of flowers) | boeket (het) | [bu'kɛt] |

| rose (flower) | roos (de) | [rõs] |
| tulip | tulp (de) | [tʉlp] |
| carnation | anjer (de) | ['anjer] |
| gladiolus | gladiool (de) | [xladi'õl] |

| cornflower | korenbloem (de) | ['kɔrənblum] |
| harebell | klokje (het) | ['klɔkjə] |
| dandelion | paardenbloem (de) | ['pārdən·blum] |
| camomile | kamille (de) | [ka'milə] |

| aloe | aloë (de) | [a'lɔe] |
| cactus | cactus (de) | ['kaktʉs] |
| rubber plant, ficus | ficus (de) | ['fikʉs] |

| lily | lelie (de) | ['leli] |
| geranium | geranium (de) | [xə'ranijum] |
| hyacinth | hyacint (de) | [hia'sint] |

| mimosa | mimosa (de) | [mi'mɔza] |
| narcissus | narcis (de) | [nar'sis] |
| nasturtium | Oostindische kers (de) | [õst 'indisə kɛrs] |

| orchid | orchidee (de) | [ɔrxi'dē] |
| peony | pioenroos (de) | [pi'un·rõs] |
| violet | viooltje (het) | [vi'jõltʃə] |

| pansy | driekleurig viooltje (het) | [dri'klørəx vi'õltʃə] |
| forget-me-not | vergeet-mij-nietje (het) | [vər'xēt-mɛj-'nitʃə] |
| daisy | madeliefje (het) | [madɛ'lifʲə] |

| poppy | papaver (de) | [pa'pavər] |
| hemp | hennep (de) | ['hɛnəp] |
| mint | munt (de) | [mʉnt] |

| lily of the valley | lelietje-van-dalen (het) | ['leljetʃə-van-'dalən] |
| snowdrop | sneeuwklokje (het) | ['snēw·'klɔkjə] |

| nettle | brandnetel (de) | ['brant·netəl] |
| sorrel | veldzuring (de) | [vɛlt·'tsʉriŋ] |
| water lily | waterlelie (de) | ['watər·leli] |
| fern | varen (de) | ['varən] |
| lichen | korstmos (het) | ['kɔrstmɔs] |

| greenhouse (tropical ~) | oranjerie (de) | [ɔranʒɛ'ri] |
| lawn | gazon (het) | [xa'zɔn] |
| flowerbed | bloemperk (het) | ['blum·pɛrk] |

| plant | plant (de) | [plant] |
| grass | gras (het) | [xras] |
| blade of grass | grasspriet (de) | ['xras·sprit] |

| leaf | blad (het) | [blat] |
| petal | bloemblad (het) | ['blum·blat] |
| stem | stengel (de) | ['stɛŋəl] |
| tuber | knol (de) | [knɔl] |

| young plant (shoot) | scheut (de) | [sxøt] |
| thorn | doorn (de) | [dõrn] |

| to blossom (vi) | bloeien | ['blujən] |
| to fade, to wither | verwelken | [vər'wɛlkən] |
| smell (odor) | geur (de) | [xør] |
| to cut (flowers) | snijden | ['snɛjdən] |
| to pick (a flower) | plukken | ['plʉkən] |

## 98. Cereals, grains

| grain | graan (het) | [xrān] |
| cereal crops | graangewassen | ['xrān·xɛ'wasən] |
| ear (of barley, etc.) | aar (de) | [ār] |

| wheat | tarwe (de) | ['tarwə] |
| rye | rogge (de) | ['rɔxə] |
| oats | haver (de) | ['havər] |

| millet | gierst (de) | [xirst] |
| barley | gerst (de) | [xɛrst] |

| corn | maïs (de) | [majs] |
| rice | rijst (de) | [rɛjst] |
| buckwheat | boekweit (de) | ['bukwɛjt] |

| pea plant | erwt (de) | [ɛrt] |
| kidney bean | boon (de) | [bõn] |
| soy | soja (de) | ['sɔja] |
| lentil | linze (de) | ['linzə] |
| beans (pulse crops) | bonen | ['bonən] |

# COUNTRIES OF
# THE WORLD

**T&P Books Publishing**

| | | |
|---|---|---|
| Afghanistan | **Afghanistan (het)** | [afˈxanistan] |
| Albania | **Albanië (het)** | [alˈbaniə] |
| Argentina | **Argentinië (het)** | [arxɛnˈtiniə] |
| Armenia | **Armenië (het)** | [arˈmeniə] |
| Australia | **Australië (het)** | [ɔuˈstraliə] |
| Austria | **Oostenrijk (het)** | [ˈõstənrɛjk] |
| Azerbaijan | **Azerbeidzjan (het)** | [azərbejˈdʒan] |
| | | |
| The Bahamas | **Bahama's** | [baˈhamas] |
| Bangladesh | **Bangladesh (het)** | [banhlaˈdɛʃ] |
| Belarus | **Wit-Rusland (het)** | [wit-ˈrʉslant] |
| Belgium | **België (het)** | [ˈbɛlxiə] |
| Bolivia | **Bolivia (het)** | [bɔˈlivia] |
| Bosnia and Herzegovina | **Bosnië** | [ˈbɔsniə |
| | **en Herzegovina (het)** | ən hɛrzəˈxɔvina] |
| Brazil | **Brazilië (het)** | [braˈziliə] |
| Bulgaria | **Bulgarije (het)** | [bʉlxaˈrɛjə] |
| | | |
| Cambodia | **Cambodja (het)** | [kamˈbɔdja] |
| Canada | **Canada (het)** | [ˈkanada] |
| Chile | **Chili (het)** | [ˈʃili] |
| China | **China (het)** | [ˈʃina] |
| Colombia | **Colombia (het)** | [kɔˈlɔmbia] |
| Croatia | **Kroatië (het)** | [krɔˈasiə] |
| Cuba | **Cuba (het)** | [ˈkʉba] |
| Cyprus | **Cyprus (het)** | [ˈsiprʉs] |
| Czech Republic | **Tsjechië (het)** | [ˈtʃɛxiə] |
| | | |
| Denmark | **Denemarken (het)** | [ˈdenəmarkən] |
| Dominican Republic | **Dominicaanse** | [dɔminiˈkãnsə |
| | **Republiek (de)** | repʉˈblik] |
| Ecuador | **Ecuador (het)** | [ɛkwaˈdɔr] |
| Egypt | **Egypte (het)** | [ɛˈxiptə] |
| England | **Engeland (het)** | [ˈɛŋɛlant] |
| Estonia | **Estland (het)** | [ˈɛstlant] |
| Finland | **Finland (het)** | [ˈfinlant] |
| France | **Frankrijk (het)** | [ˈfrankrɛjk] |
| French Polynesia | **Frans-Polynesië** | [frans-pɔliˈnɛziə] |
| | | |
| Georgia | **Georgië (het)** | [xeˈorxiə] |
| Germany | **Duitsland (het)** | [ˈdœʏtslant] |
| Ghana | **Ghana (het)** | [ˈxana] |
| Great Britain | **Groot-Brittannië (het)** | [xrõt-briˈtaniə] |
| Greece | **Griekenland (het)** | [ˈxrikənlant] |

| Haiti | **Haïti (het)** | [ha'iti] |
| Hungary | **Hongarije (het)** | [hɔnxa'rɛjə] |

## 100. Countries. Part 2

| Iceland | **IJsland (het)** | ['ɛjslant] |
| India | **India (het)** | ['india] |
| Indonesia | **Indonesië (het)** | [indɔ'nɛsiə] |
| Iran | **Iran (het)** | [i'ran] |
| Iraq | **Irak (het)** | [i'rak] |
| Ireland | **Ierland (het)** | ['īrlant] |
| Israel | **Israël (het)** | ['israɛl] |
| Italy | **Italië (het)** | [i'taliə] |

| Jamaica | **Jamaica (het)** | [ja'majka] |
| Japan | **Japan (het)** | [ja'pan] |
| Jordan | **Jordanië (het)** | [jor'daniə] |
| Kazakhstan | **Kazakstan (het)** | [kazak'stan] |
| Kenya | **Kenia (het)** | ['kenia] |
| Kirghizia | **Kirgizië (het)** | [kir'xiziə] |
| Kuwait | **Koeweit (het)** | [ku'wɛjt] |

| Laos | **Laos (het)** | ['laɔs] |
| Latvia | **Letland (het)** | ['lɛtlant] |
| Lebanon | **Libanon (het)** | ['libanɔn] |
| Libya | **Libië (het)** | ['libiə] |
| Liechtenstein | **Liechtenstein (het)** | ['lixtɛnstɛjn] |
| Lithuania | **Litouwen (het)** | [li'tauən] |
| Luxembourg | **Luxemburg (het)** | ['lʉksɛmbʉrx] |

| Macedonia (Republic of ~) | **Macedonië (het)** | [make'dɔniə] |
| Madagascar | **Madagaskar (het)** | [mada'xaskar] |
| Malaysia | **Maleisië (het)** | [ma'lɛjziə] |
| Malta | **Malta (het)** | ['malta] |
| Mexico | **Mexico (het)** | ['meksikɔ] |
| Moldova, Moldavia | **Moldavië (het)** | [mɔl'daviə] |

| Monaco | **Monaco (het)** | [mɔ'nakɔ] |
| Mongolia | **Mongolië (het)** | [mɔn'xɔliə] |
| Montenegro | **Montenegro (het)** | [mɔntə'nɛxrɔ] |

| Morocco | **Marokko (het)** | [ma'rɔkɔ] |
| Myanmar | **Myanmar (het)** | ['mjanmar] |

| Namibia | **Namibië (het)** | [na'mibiə] |
| Nepal | **Nepal (het)** | [ne'pal] |
| Netherlands | **Nederland (het)** | ['nedərlant] |
| New Zealand | **Nieuw-Zeeland (het)** | [niu-'zēlant] |
| North Korea | **Noord-Korea (het)** | [nōrd-kɔ'rea] |
| Norway | **Noorwegen (het)** | ['nōrwexən] |

## 101. Countries. Part 3

| | | |
|---|---|---|
| Pakistan | Pakistan (het) | ['pakistan] |
| Palestine | Palestijnse autonomie (de) | [pale'stɛjnsə autɔno'mi] |
| Panama | Panama (het) | ['panama] |
| Paraguay | Paraguay (het) | ['paragvaj] |
| Peru | Peru (het) | [pe'ru] |
| Poland | Polen (het) | ['pɔlən] |
| Portugal | Portugal (het) | [pɔrtʉxal] |
| Romania | Roemenië (het) | [ru'meniə] |
| Russia | Rusland (het) | ['rʉslant] |
| | | |
| Saudi Arabia | Saoedi-Arabië (het) | [sa'udi-a'rabiə] |
| Scotland | Schotland (het) | ['sxɔtlant] |
| Senegal | Senegal (het) | [senexal] |
| Serbia | Servië (het) | ['sɛrviə] |
| Slovakia | Slowakije (het) | [slɔwa'kɛjə] |
| Slovenia | Slovenië (het) | [slɔ'vɛniə] |
| | | |
| South Africa | Zuid-Afrika (het) | ['zœʏd-'afrika] |
| South Korea | Zuid-Korea (het) | ['zœʏd-kɔ'rea] |
| Spain | Spanje (het) | ['spanjə] |
| Suriname | Suriname (het) | [sʉri'namə] |
| Sweden | Zweden (het) | ['zwedən] |
| Switzerland | Zwitserland (het) | ['zwitsərlant] |
| Syria | Syrië (het) | ['siriə] |
| | | |
| Taiwan | Taiwan (het) | [taj'wan] |
| Tajikistan | Tadzjikistan (het) | [ta'dʒikistan] |
| Tanzania | Tanzania (het) | [tan'zania] |
| Tasmania | Tasmanië (het) | [taz'maniə] |
| Thailand | Thailand (het) | ['tailant] |
| Tunisia | Tunesië (het) | [tʉ'nɛziə] |
| Turkey | Turkije (het) | [tʉr'kɛjə] |
| Turkmenistan | Turkmenistan (het) | [tʉrk'menistan] |
| | | |
| Ukraine | Oekraïne (het) | [ukra'inə] |
| United Arab Emirates | Verenigde Arabische Emiraten | [və'rɛnixdə a'rabisə ɛmi'ratən] |
| United States of America | Verenigde Staten van Amerika | [və'rɛnixdə 'statən van a'merika] |
| Uruguay | Uruguay (het) | ['urugvaj] |
| Uzbekistan | Oezbekistan (het) | [uz'bekistan] |
| | | |
| Vatican | Vaticaanstad (de) | [vati'kãn·stat] |
| Venezuela | Venezuela (het) | [venəzʉ'ɛla] |
| Vietnam | Vietnam (het) | [vjet'nam] |
| Zanzibar | Zanzibar (het) | ['zanzibar] |

# GASTRONOMIC GLOSSARY

This section contains a lot of
words and terms associated
with food. This dictionary will
make it easier for you to
understand the menu at a
restaurant and choose
the right dish

**T&P Books Publishing**

| | | |
|---|---|---|
| aftertaste | nasmaak (de) | ['nasmāk] |
| almond | amandel (de) | [a'mandəl] |
| anise | anijs (de) | [a'nɛjs] |
| aperitif | aperitief (de/het) | [aperi'tif] |
| appetite | eetlust (de) | ['ētlʊst] |
| appetizer | voorgerecht (het) | ['vōrxərɛht] |
| apple | appel (de) | ['apəl] |
| apricot | abrikoos (de) | [abri'kōs] |
| artichoke | artisjok (de) | [arti'ɕɔk] |
| asparagus | asperge (de) | [as'pɛrʒə] |
| Atlantic salmon | atlantische zalm (de) | [at'lantisə zalm] |
| avocado | avocado (de) | [avɔ'kadɔ] |
| bacon | spek (het) | [spɛk] |
| banana | banaan (de) | [ba'nān] |
| barley | gerst (de) | [xɛrst] |
| bartender | barman (de) | ['barman] |
| basil | basilicum (de) | [ba'silikəm] |
| bay leaf | laurierblad (het) | [lau'rir·blat] |
| beans | bonen | ['bɔnən] |
| beef | rundvlees (het) | ['rʊnt·vlēs] |
| beer | bier (het) | [bir] |
| beetroot | rode biet (de) | ['rɔdə bit] |
| bell pepper | peper (de) | ['pepər] |
| berries | bessen | ['bɛsən] |
| berry | bes (de) | [bɛs] |
| bilberry | bosbes (de) | ['bɔsbɛs] |
| birch bolete | berkenboleet (de) | ['bɛrkən·bɔlēt] |
| bitter | bitter | ['bitər] |
| black coffee | zwarte koffie (de) | ['zwartə 'kɔfi] |
| black pepper | zwarte peper (de) | ['zwartə 'pepər] |
| black tea | zwarte thee (de) | ['zwartə tē] |
| blackberry | braambes (de) | ['brāmbɛs] |
| blackcurrant | zwarte bes (de) | ['zwartə bɛs] |
| boiled | gekookt | [xə'kōkt] |
| bottle opener | flesopener (de) | [fles·'ɔpənər] |
| bread | brood (het) | [brōt] |
| breakfast | ontbijt (het) | [ɔn'bɛjt] |
| bream | brasem (de) | ['brasəm] |
| broccoli | broccoli (de) | ['brɔkɔli] |
| Brussels sprouts | spruitkool (de) | ['sprœʏt·kōl] |
| buckwheat | boekweit (de) | ['bukwɛjt] |
| butter | boter (de) | ['bɔtər] |
| buttercream | crème (de) | [krɛːm] |
| cabbage | kool (de) | [kōl] |

| | | |
|---|---|---|
| cake | cakeje (het) | ['kejkjə] |
| cake | taart (de) | [tārt] |
| calorie | calorie (de) | [kalɔ'ri] |
| can opener | blikopener (de) | [blik·'ɔpənər] |
| candy | snoepje (het) | ['snupjə] |
| canned food | conserven | [kɔn'sɛrvən] |
| cappuccino | cappuccino (de) | [kapu'ʧinɔ] |
| caraway | komijn (de) | [kɔ'mɛjn] |
| carbohydrates | koolhydraten | [kōlhi'dratən] |
| carbonated | koolzuurhoudend | [kōlzūr·'haudənt] |
| carp | karper (de) | ['karpər] |
| carrot | wortel (de) | ['wɔrtəl] |
| catfish | meerval (de) | ['mērval] |
| cauliflower | bloemkool (de) | ['blum·kōl] |
| caviar | kaviaar (de) | [ka'vjār] |
| celery | selderij (de) | ['sɛldɛrɛj] |
| cep | gewoon eekhoorntjesbrood (het) | [xə'wōn ē'hɔntʃes·brōt] |
| cereal crops | graangewassen | ['xrān·xɛ'wasən] |
| cereal grains | graan (het) | [xrān] |
| champagne | champagne (de) | [ʃʌm'panjə] |
| chanterelle | cantharel (de) | [kanta'rɛl] |
| check | rekening (de) | ['rekəniŋ] |
| cheese | kaas (de) | [kās] |
| chewing gum | kauwgom (de) | ['kauxɔm] |
| chicken | kip (de) | [kip] |
| chocolate | chocolade (de) | [ʃɔkɔ'ladə] |
| chocolate | chocolade- | [ʃɔkɔ'ladə] |
| cinnamon | kaneel (de/het) | [ka'nēl] |
| clear soup | bouillon (de) | [bu'jon] |
| cloves | kruidnagel (de) | ['krœʏtnaxəl] |
| cocktail | cocktail (de) | ['kɔktəl] |
| coconut | kokosnoot (de) | ['kɔkɔs·nōt] |
| cod | kabeljauw (de) | [kabə'ljau] |
| coffee | koffie (de) | ['kɔfi] |
| coffee with milk | koffie (de) met melk | ['kɔfi mɛt mɛlk] |
| cognac | cognac (de) | [kɔ'njak] |
| cold | koud | ['kaut] |
| condensed milk | gecondenseerde melk (de) | [xəkɔnsən'sērdə mɛlk] |
| condiment | condiment (het) | [kɔndi'mɛnt] |
| confectionery | suikerbakkerij (de) | [sœʏkər bakə'rɛj] |
| cookies | koekje (het) | ['kukjə] |
| coriander | koriander (de) | [kɔri'andər] |
| corkscrew | kurkentrekker (de) | ['kʉrkən·'trɛkər] |
| corn | maïs (de) | [majs] |
| corn | maïs (de) | [majs] |
| cornflakes | maïsvlokken | [majs·'vlɔkən] |
| course, dish | gerecht (het) | [xe'rɛht] |
| cowberry | vossenbes (de) | ['vɔsənbɛs] |
| crab | krab (de) | [krab] |
| cranberry | veenbes (de) | ['vēnbɛs] |

| | | |
|---|---|---|
| cream | room (de) | [rōm] |
| crumb | kruimel (de) | ['krœʏməl] |
| crustaceans | schaaldieren | ['sxal·dīrən] |
| cucumber | augurk (de) | [au'xʏrk] |
| cuisine | keuken (de) | ['køkən] |
| cup | kopje (het) | ['kɔpjə] |
| dark beer | donker bier (het) | ['dɔnkər bir] |
| date | dadel (de) | ['dadəl] |
| death cap | groene knolamaniet (de) | ['xrunə 'knɔl·ama'nit] |
| dessert | dessert (het) | [dɛ'sɛːr] |
| diet | dieet (het) | [di'ēt] |
| dill | dille (de) | ['dilə] |
| dinner | avondeten (het) | ['avɔntetən] |
| dried | gedroogd | [xə'drōxt] |
| drinking water | drinkwater (het) | ['drink·'watər] |
| duck | eend (de) | [ēnt] |
| ear | aar (de) | [ār] |
| edible mushroom | eetbare paddenstoel (de) | ['ētbarə 'padənstul] |
| eel | paling (de) | [pa'liŋ] |
| egg | ei (het) | [ɛj] |
| egg white | eiwit (het) | ['ɛjwit] |
| egg yolk | eigeel (het) | ['ɛjxēl] |
| eggplant | aubergine (de) | [ɔbɛr'ʒinə] |
| eggs | eieren | ['ɛjerən] |
| Enjoy your meal! | Eet smakelijk! | [ēt 'smakələk] |
| fats | vetten | ['vɛtən] |
| fig | vijg (de) | [vɛjx] |
| filling | vulling (de) | ['vʉliŋ] |
| fish | vis (de) | [vis] |
| flatfish | platvis (de) | ['platvis] |
| flour | meel (het), bloem (de) | [mēl], [blum] |
| fly agaric | vliegenzwam (de) | ['vlixən·zwam] |
| food | eten (het) | ['etən] |
| fork | vork (de) | [vɔrk] |
| freshly squeezed juice | vers geperst sap (het) | [vɛrs xə'pɛrst sap] |
| fried | gebakken | [xə'bakən] |
| fried eggs | spiegelei (het) | ['spixəl·ɛj] |
| frozen | diepvries | ['dip·vris] |
| fruit | vrucht (de) | [vrʉxt] |
| fruits | vruchten | ['vrʉxtən] |
| game | wild (het) | [wilt] |
| gammon | gerookte achterham (de) | [xə'rōktə 'ahtərham] |
| garlic | knoflook (de) | ['knõflɔk] |
| gin | gin (de) | [dʒin] |
| ginger | gember (de) | ['xɛmbər] |
| glass | glas (het) | [xlas] |
| glass | wijnglas (het) | ['wɛjn·xlas] |
| goose | gans (de) | [xans] |
| gooseberry | kruisbes (de) | ['krœʏsbɛs] |
| grain | graan (het) | [xrān] |
| grape | druif (de) | [drœʏf] |
| grapefruit | grapefruit (de) | ['grepfrut] |

| green tea | groene thee (de) | ['xrunə tē] |
| greens | verse kruiden | ['vɛrsə 'krœydən] |
| halibut | heilbot (de) | ['hɛjlbɔt] |
| ham | ham (de) | [ham] |
| hamburger | gehakt (het) | [xə'hakt] |
| hamburger | hamburger (de) | ['hambʉrxər] |
| hazelnut | hazelnoot (de) | ['hazəl·nōt] |
| herring | haring (de) | ['hariŋ] |
| honey | honing (de) | ['hɔniŋ] |
| horseradish | mierikswortel (de) | ['miriks·'wɔrtəl] |
| hot | heet | [hēt] |
| ice | ijs (het) | [ɛjs] |
| ice-cream | ijsje (het) | ['ɛisjə], ['ɛiʃə] |
| instant coffee | oploskoffie (de) | ['ɔplɔs·'kɔfi] |
| jam | jam (de) | [ʃɛm] |
| jam | confituur (de) | [kɔnfi'tūr] |
| juice | sap (het) | [sap] |
| kidney bean | boon (de) | [bōn] |
| kiwi | kiwi (de) | ['kiwi] |
| knife | mes (het) | [mɛs] |
| lamb | schapenvlees (het) | ['sxapən·vlēs] |
| lemon | citroen (de) | [si'trun] |
| lemonade | limonade (de) | [limɔ'nadə] |
| lentil | linze (de) | ['linzə] |
| lettuce | sla (de) | [sla] |
| light beer | licht bier (het) | [lixt bir] |
| liqueur | likeur (de) | [li'kør] |
| liquors | alcoholische dranken | [alkɔ'hɔlisə 'drankən] |
| liver | lever (de) | ['levər] |
| lunch | lunch (de) | ['lunʃ] |
| mackerel | makreel (de) | [ma'krēl] |
| mandarin | mandarijn (de) | [manda'rɛjn] |
| mango | mango (de) | ['mangɔ] |
| margarine | margarine (de) | [marxa'rinə] |
| marmalade | marmelade (de) | [marmə'ladə] |
| mashed potatoes | aardappelpuree (de) | ['ārdapəl·pʉ'rē] |
| mayonnaise | mayonaise (de) | [majo'nɛzə] |
| meat | vlees (het) | [vlēs] |
| melon | meloen (de) | [mə'lun] |
| menu | menu (het) | [me'nʉ] |
| milk | melk (de) | [mɛlk] |
| milkshake | milkshake (de) | ['milk·ʃɛjk] |
| millet | gierst (de) | [xirst] |
| mineral water | mineraalwater (het) | [minə'rāl·'watər] |
| morel | morielje (de) | [mɔ'riljə] |
| mushroom | paddenstoel (de) | ['padənstul] |
| mustard | mosterd (de) | ['mɔstərt] |
| non-alcoholic | alcohol vrij | ['alkɔhɔl vrɛj] |
| noodles | noedels | ['nudɛls] |
| oats | haver (de) | ['havər] |
| olive oil | olijfolie (de) | [ɔ'lɛjf·'ɔli] |

| | | |
|---|---|---|
| olives | olijven | [ɔ'lɛjvən] |
| omelet | omelet (de) | [ɔmə'lɛt] |
| onion | ui (de) | ['œʏ] |
| orange | sinaasappel (de) | ['sināsapəl] |
| orange juice | sinaasappelsap (het) | ['sināsapəl·sap] |
| orange-cap boletus | rosse populierenboleet (de) | ['rɔsə pɔpʉ'lirən·bɔlēt] |
| oyster | oester (de) | ['ustər] |
| pâté | paté (de) | [pa'tɛ] |
| papaya | papaja (de) | [pa'paja] |
| paprika | paprika (de) | ['paprika] |
| parsley | peterselie (de) | [petər'sɛli] |
| pasta | pasta (de) | ['pasta] |
| pea | erwt (de) | [ɛrt] |
| peach | perzik (de) | ['pɛrzik] |
| peanut | pinda (de) | ['pinda] |
| pear | peer (de) | [pēr] |
| peel | schil (de) | [sxil] |
| perch | baars (de) | [bārs] |
| pickled | gemarineerd | [xəmari'nērt] |
| pie | pastei (de) | [pas'tɛj] |
| piece | stuk (het) | [stʉk] |
| pike | snoek (de) | [snuk] |
| pike perch | snoekbaars (de) | ['snukbārs] |
| pineapple | ananas (de) | ['ananas] |
| pistachios | pistaches | [pi'staʃəs] |
| pizza | pizza (de) | ['pitsa] |
| plate | bord (het) | [bɔrt] |
| plum | pruim (de) | ['prœʏm] |
| poisonous mushroom | giftige paddenstoel (de) | ['xiftixə 'padənstul] |
| pomegranate | granaatappel (de) | [xra'nāt·'apəl] |
| pork | varkensvlees (het) | ['varkəns·vlēs] |
| porridge | pap (de) | [pap] |
| portion | portie (de) | ['pɔrsi] |
| potato | aardappel (de) | ['ārd·apəl] |
| proteins | eiwitten | ['ɛjwitən] |
| pub, bar | bar (de) | [bar] |
| pudding | pudding (de) | ['pʉdiŋ] |
| pumpkin | pompoen (de) | [pɔm'pun] |
| rabbit | konijnenvlees (het) | [kɔ'nɛjnən·vlēs] |
| radish | radijs (de) | [ra'dɛjs] |
| raisin | rozijn (de) | [rɔ'zɛjn] |
| raspberry | framboos (de) | [fram'bōs] |
| recipe | recept (het) | [re'sɛpt] |
| red pepper | rode peper (de) | ['rɔdə 'pepər] |
| red wine | rode wijn (de) | ['rɔdə wɛjn] |
| redcurrant | rode bes (de) | ['rɔdə bɛs] |
| refreshing drink | frisdrank (de) | ['fris·drank] |
| rice | rijst (de) | [rɛjst] |
| rum | rum (de) | [rʉm] |
| russula | russula (de) | [rʉ'sʉla] |
| rye | rogge (de) | ['rɔxə] |

| | | |
|---|---|---|
| saffron | **saffraan (de)** | [saf'rān] |
| salad | **salade (de)** | [sa'ladə] |
| salmon | **zalm (de)** | [zalm] |
| salt | **zout (het)** | ['zaut] |
| salty | **gezouten** | [xə'zautən] |
| sandwich | **boterham (de)** | ['botərham] |
| sardine | **sardine (de)** | [sar'dinə] |
| sauce | **saus (de)** | ['saus] |
| saucer | **schoteltje (het)** | ['sxɔteltʃə] |
| sausage | **worst (de)** | [wɔrst] |
| seafood | **zeevruchten** | [zē·'vrʉxtən] |
| sesame | **sesamzaad (het)** | ['sɛzam·zāt] |
| shark | **haai (de)** | [hāj] |
| shrimp | **garnaal (de)** | [xar'nāl] |
| side dish | **garnering (de)** | [xar'neriŋ] |
| slice | **snede (de)** | ['snedə] |
| smoked | **gerookt** | [xə'rōkt] |
| soft drink | **alcohol vrije drank (de)** | ['alkɔhɔl 'vrɛjə drank] |
| soup | **soep (de)** | [sup] |
| soup spoon | **eetlepel (de)** | [ēt·'lepəl] |
| sour cherry | **zure kers (de)** | ['zʉrə kɛrs] |
| sour cream | **zure room (de)** | ['zʉrə rōm] |
| soy | **soja (de)** | ['sɔja] |
| spaghetti | **spaghetti (de)** | [spa'xeti] |
| sparkling | **bruisend** | ['brœysənt] |
| spice | **specerij , kruiderij (de)** | [spesə'rɛj], [krœyda'rɛj] |
| spinach | **spinazie (de)** | [spi'nazi] |
| spiny lobster | **langoest (de)** | [lan'xust] |
| spoon | **lepel (de)** | ['lepəl] |
| squid | **inktvis (de)** | ['inktvis] |
| steak | **biefstuk (de)** | ['bifstʉk] |
| still | **zonder gas** | ['zɔndər xas] |
| strawberry | **aardbei (de)** | ['ārd·bɛj] |
| sturgeon | **steur (de)** | ['stør] |
| sugar | **suiker (de)** | ['sœykər] |
| sunflower oil | **zonnebloemolie (de)** | ['zɔnəblum·'ɔli] |
| sweet | **zoet** | [zut] |
| sweet cherry | **zoete kers (de)** | ['zutə kɛrs] |
| taste, flavor | **smaak (de)** | [smāk] |
| tasty | **lekker** | ['lɛkər] |
| tea | **thee (de)** | [tē] |
| teaspoon | **theelepeltje (het)** | [tē·'lepəltʃə] |
| tip | **fooi (de)** | [fōj] |
| tomato | **tomaat (de)** | [tɔ'māt] |
| tomato juice | **tomatensap (het)** | [tɔ'matən·sap] |
| tongue | **tong (de)** | [tɔŋ] |
| toothpick | **tandenstoker (de)** | ['tandən·'stɔkər] |
| trout | **forel (de)** | [fɔ'rɛl] |
| tuna | **tonijn (de)** | [tɔ'nɛjn] |
| turkey | **kalkoen (de)** | [kal'kun] |
| turnip | **raap (de)** | [rāp] |
| veal | **kalfsvlees (het)** | ['kalfs·vlēs] |

| vegetable oil | plantaardige olie (de) | [plant'ārdixə 'ɔli] |
| vegetables | groenten | ['xruntən] |
| vegetarian | vegetariër (de) | [vəxɛ'tarier] |
| vegetarian | vegetarisch | [vəxɛ'taris] |
| vermouth | vermout (de) | ['vɛrmut] |
| vienna sausage | saucijs (de) | ['sɔsɛjs] |
| vinegar | azijn (de) | [a'zɛjn] |
| vitamin | vitamine (de) | [vita'minə] |
| vodka | wodka (de) | ['wɔdka] |
| waffles | wafel (de) | ['wafəl] |
| waiter | kelner, ober (de) | ['kɛlnər], ['ɔbər] |
| waitress | serveerster (de) | [sɛr'vērstər] |
| walnut | walnoot (de) | ['walnõt] |
| water | water (het) | ['watər] |
| watermelon | watermeloen (de) | ['watərmɛ'lun] |
| wheat | tarwe (de) | ['tarwə] |
| whiskey | whisky (de) | ['wiski] |
| white wine | witte wijn (de) | ['witə wɛjn] |
| wild strawberry | bosaardbei (de) | [bɔs·ārdbɛj] |
| wine | wijn (de) | [wɛjn] |
| wine list | wijnkaart (de) | ['wɛjn·kãrt] |
| with ice | met ijs | [mɛt ɛjs] |
| yogurt | yoghurt (de) | ['jogurt] |
| zucchini | courgette (de) | [kur'ʒɛt] |

# Dutch-English gastronomic glossary

| | | |
|---|---|---|
| aar (de) | [ār] | ear |
| aardappel (de) | ['ārd·apəl] | potato |
| aardappelpuree (de) | ['ārdapəl·pʉ'rē] | mashed potatoes |
| aardbei (de) | ['ārd·bɛj] | strawberry |
| abrikoos (de) | [abri'kōs] | apricot |
| alcohol vrij | ['alkɔhɔl vrɛj] | non-alcoholic |
| alcohol vrije drank (de) | ['alkɔhɔl 'vrɛjə drank] | soft drink |
| alcoholische dranken | [alkɔ'hɔlisə 'drankən] | liquors |
| amandel (de) | [a'mandəl] | almond |
| ananas (de) | ['ananas] | pineapple |
| anijs (de) | [a'nɛjs] | anise |
| aperitief (de/het) | [aperi'tif] | aperitif |
| appel (de) | ['apəl] | apple |
| artisjok (de) | [arti'çɔk] | artichoke |
| asperge (de) | [as'pɛrʒə] | asparagus |
| atlantische zalm (de) | [at'lantisə zalm] | Atlantic salmon |
| aubergine (de) | [ɔbɛr'ʒinə] | eggplant |
| augurk (de) | [au'xʉrk] | cucumber |
| avocado (de) | [avɔ'kadɔ] | avocado |
| avondeten (het) | ['avɔntetən] | dinner |
| azijn (de) | [a'zɛjn] | vinegar |
| baars (de) | [bārs] | perch |
| banaan (de) | [ba'nān] | banana |
| bar (de) | [bar] | pub, bar |
| barman (de) | ['barman] | bartender |
| basilicum (de) | [ba'silikəm] | basil |
| berkenboleet (de) | ['bɛrkən·bɔlēt] | birch bolete |
| bes (de) | [bɛs] | berry |
| bessen | ['bɛsən] | berries |
| biefstuk (de) | ['bifstʉk] | steak |
| bier (het) | [bir] | beer |
| bitter | ['bitər] | bitter |
| blikopener (de) | [blik·'ɔpənər] | can opener |
| bloemkool (de) | ['blum·kōl] | cauliflower |
| boekweit (de) | ['bukwɛjt] | buckwheat |
| bonen | ['bonən] | beans |
| boon (de) | [bōn] | kidney bean |
| bord (het) | [bort] | plate |
| bosaardbei (de) | [bɔs·ārdbɛj] | wild strawberry |
| bosbes (de) | ['bɔsbɛs] | bilberry |
| boter (de) | ['botər] | butter |
| boterham (de) | ['botərham] | sandwich |
| bouillon (de) | [bu'jon] | clear soup |

| | | |
|---|---|---|
| braambes (de) | ['brãmbɛs] | blackberry |
| brasem (de) | ['brasəm] | bream |
| broccoli (de) | ['brɔkɔli] | broccoli |
| brood (het) | [brõt] | bread |
| bruisend | ['brœʏsənt] | sparkling |
| cakeje (het) | ['kejkje] | cake |
| calorie (de) | [kalɔ'ri] | calorie |
| cantharel (de) | [kanta'rɛl] | chanterelle |
| cappuccino (de) | [kapu'ʧinɔ] | cappuccino |
| champagne (de) | [ʃʌm'panjə] | champagne |
| chocolade (de) | [ʃɔkɔ'ladə] | chocolate |
| chocolade- | [ʃɔkɔ'ladə] | chocolate |
| citroen (de) | [si'trun] | lemon |
| cocktail (de) | ['kɔktəl] | cocktail |
| cognac (de) | [kɔ'njak] | cognac |
| condiment (het) | [kɔndi'mɛnt] | condiment |
| confituur (de) | [kɔnfi'tũr] | jam |
| conserven | [kɔn'sɛrvən] | canned food |
| courgette (de) | [kur'ʒɛt] | zucchini |
| crème (de) | [krɛ:m] | buttercream |
| dadel (de) | ['dadəl] | date |
| dessert (het) | [dɛ'sɛ:r] | dessert |
| dieet (het) | [di'ẽt] | diet |
| diepvries | ['dip·vris] | frozen |
| dille (de) | ['dilə] | dill |
| donker bier (het) | ['dɔnkər bir] | dark beer |
| drinkwater (het) | ['drink·'watər] | drinking water |
| druif (de) | [drœʏf] | grape |
| eend (de) | [ẽnt] | duck |
| Eet smakelijk! | [ẽt 'smakələk] | Enjoy your meal! |
| eetbare paddenstoel (de) | ['ẽtbarə 'padənstul] | edible mushroom |
| eetlepel (de) | [ẽt·'lepəl] | soup spoon |
| eetlust (de) | ['ẽtlʊst] | appetite |
| ei (het) | [ɛj] | egg |
| eieren | ['ɛjerən] | eggs |
| eigeel (het) | ['ɛjxẽl] | egg yolk |
| eiwit (het) | ['ɛjwit] | egg white |
| eiwitten | ['ɛjwitən] | proteins |
| erwt (de) | [ɛrt] | pea |
| eten (het) | ['etən] | food |
| flesopener (de) | [fles·'ɔpənər] | bottle opener |
| fooi (de) | [fõj] | tip |
| forel (de) | [fɔ'rɛl] | trout |
| framboos (de) | [fram'bõs] | raspberry |
| frisdrank (de) | ['fris·drank] | refreshing drink |
| gans (de) | [xans] | goose |
| garnaal (de) | [xar'nãl] | shrimp |
| garnering (de) | [xar'neriŋ] | side dish |
| gebakken | [xə'bakən] | fried |
| gecondenseerde melk | [xəkɔnsən'sẽrdə mɛlk] | condensed milk |
| gedroogd | [xə'drõxt] | dried |

| gehakt (het) | [xə'hakt] | hamburger |
| gekookt | [xə'kōkt] | boiled |
| gemarineerd | [xəmari'nērt] | pickled |
| gember (de) | ['xɛmbər] | ginger |
| gerecht (het) | [xe'rɛht] | course, dish |
| gerookt | [xə'rōkt] | smoked |
| gerookte achterham (de) | [xə'rōktə 'ahtərham] | gammon |
| gerst (de) | [xɛrst] | barley |
| gewoon eekhoorntjesbrood (het) | [xə'wōn ē'hɔntʃes·brōt] | cep |
| gezouten | [xə'zautən] | salty |
| gierst (de) | [xirst] | millet |
| giftige paddenstoel (de) | ['xiftixə 'padənstul] | poisonous mushroom |
| gin (de) | [dʒin] | gin |
| glas (het) | [xlas] | glass |
| graan (het) | [xrān] | cereal grains |
| graan (het) | [xrān] | grain |
| graangewassen | ['xrān·xɛ'wasən] | cereal crops |
| granaatappel (de) | [xra'nāt·'apəl] | pomegranate |
| grapefruit (de) | ['grepfrut] | grapefruit |
| groene knolamaniet (de) | ['xrunə 'knɔl·ama'nit] | death cap |
| groene thee (de) | ['xrunə tē] | green tea |
| groenten | ['xruntən] | vegetables |
| haai (de) | [hāj] | shark |
| ham (de) | [ham] | ham |
| hamburger (de) | ['hambʉrxər] | hamburger |
| haring (de) | ['hariŋ] | herring |
| haver (de) | ['havər] | oats |
| hazelnoot (de) | ['hazəl·nōt] | hazelnut |
| heet | [hēt] | hot |
| heilbot (de) | ['hɛjlbɔt] | halibut |
| honing (de) | ['hɔniŋ] | honey |
| ijs (het) | [ɛjs] | ice |
| ijsje (het) | ['ɛisjə], ['ɛiʃə] | ice-cream |
| inktvis (de) | ['inktvis] | squid |
| jam (de) | [ʃɛm] | jam |
| kaas (de) | [kās] | cheese |
| kabeljauw (de) | [kabə'ljau] | cod |
| kalfsvlees (het) | ['kalfs·vlēs] | veal |
| kalkoen (de) | [kal'kun] | turkey |
| kaneel (de/het) | [ka'nēl] | cinnamon |
| karper (de) | ['karpər] | carp |
| kauwgom (de) | ['kauxɔm] | chewing gum |
| kaviaar (de) | [ka'vjār] | caviar |
| kelner, ober (de) | ['kɛlnər], ['ɔbər] | waiter |
| keuken (de) | ['køkən] | cuisine |
| kip (de) | [kip] | chicken |
| kiwi (de) | ['kiwi] | kiwi |
| knoflook (de) | ['knōflɔk] | garlic |
| koekje (het) | ['kukjə] | cookies |
| koffie (de) | ['kɔfi] | coffee |
| koffie (de) met melk | ['kɔfi mɛt mɛlk] | coffee with milk |

| | | |
|---|---|---|
| kokosnoot (de) | ['kɔkɔs·nõt] | coconut |
| komijn (de) | [kɔ'mɛjn] | caraway |
| konijnenvlees (het) | [kɔ'nɛjnən·vlēs] | rabbit |
| kool (de) | [kõl] | cabbage |
| koolhydraten | [kõlhi'dratən] | carbohydrates |
| koolzuurhoudend | [kõlzũr·'haudənt] | carbonated |
| kopje (het) | ['kɔpjə] | cup |
| koriander (de) | [kɔri'andər] | coriander |
| koud | ['kaut] | cold |
| krab (de) | [krab] | crab |
| kruidnagel (de) | ['krœʏtnaxəl] | cloves |
| kruimel (de) | ['krœʏməl] | crumb |
| kruisbes (de) | ['krœʏsbɛs] | gooseeberry |
| kurkentrekker (de) | ['kʉrkən·'trɛkər] | corkscrew |
| langoest (de) | [lan'xust] | spiny lobster |
| laurierblad (het) | [lau'rir·blat] | bay leaf |
| lekker | ['lɛkər] | tasty |
| lepel (de) | ['lepəl] | spoon |
| lever (de) | ['levər] | liver |
| licht bier (het) | [lixt bir] | light beer |
| likeur (de) | [li'kør] | liqueur |
| limonade (de) | [limɔ'nadə] | lemonade |
| linze (de) | ['linzə] | lentil |
| lunch (de) | ['lʉnʃ] | lunch |
| maïs (de) | [majs] | corn |
| maïs (de) | [majs] | corn |
| maïsvlokken | [majs·'vlɔkən] | cornflakes |
| makreel (de) | [ma'krēl] | mackerel |
| mandarijn (de) | [manda'rɛjn] | mandarin |
| mango (de) | ['mangɔ] | mango |
| margarine (de) | [marxa'rinə] | margarine |
| marmelade (de) | [marmə'ladə] | marmalade |
| mayonaise (de) | [majɔ'nɛzə] | mayonnaise |
| meel (het), bloem (de) | [mēl], [blum] | flour |
| meerval (de) | ['mērval] | catfish |
| melk (de) | [mɛlk] | milk |
| meloen (de) | [mə'lun] | melon |
| menu (het) | [me'nʉ] | menu |
| mes (het) | [mɛs] | knife |
| met ijs | [mɛt ɛjs] | with ice |
| mierikswortel (de) | ['miriks·'wɔrtəl] | horseradish |
| milkshake (de) | ['milk·ʃɛjk] | milkshake |
| mineraalwater (het) | [minə'rāl·'watər] | mineral water |
| morielje (de) | [mɔ'riljə] | morel |
| mosterd (de) | ['mɔstərt] | mustard |
| nasmaak (de) | ['nasmāk] | aftertaste |
| noedels | ['nudɛls] | noodles |
| oester (de) | ['ustər] | oyster |
| olijfolie (de) | [ɔ'lɛjf·'ɔli] | olive oil |
| olijven | [ɔ'lɛjvən] | olives |
| omelet (de) | [ɔmə'lɛt] | omelet |
| ontbijt (het) | [ɔn'bɛjt] | breakfast |

| | | |
|---|---|---|
| oploskoffie (de) | ['ɔplɔs·'kɔfi] | instant coffee |
| paddenstoel (de) | ['padənstul] | mushroom |
| paling (de) | [pa'liŋ] | eel |
| pap (de) | [pap] | porridge |
| papaja (de) | [pa'paja] | papaya |
| paprika (de) | ['paprika] | paprika |
| pasta (de) | ['pasta] | pasta |
| pastei (de) | [pas'tɛj] | pie |
| paté (de) | [pa'tɛ] | pâté |
| peer (de) | [pēr] | pear |
| peper (de) | ['pepər] | bell pepper |
| perzik (de) | ['pɛrzik] | peach |
| peterselie (de) | [petər'sɛli] | parsley |
| pinda (de) | ['pinda] | peanut |
| pistaches | [pi'staʃəs] | pistachios |
| pizza (de) | ['pitsa] | pizza |
| plantaardige olie (de) | [plant'ārdixə 'ɔli] | vegetable oil |
| platvis (de) | ['platvis] | flatfish |
| pompoen (de) | [pɔm'pun] | pumpkin |
| portie (de) | ['pɔrsi] | portion |
| pruim (de) | ['prœʏm] | plum |
| pudding (de) | ['pʉdiŋ] | pudding |
| raap (de) | [rāp] | turnip |
| radijs (de) | [ra'dɛjs] | radish |
| recept (het) | [re'sɛpt] | recipe |
| rekening (de) | ['rekəniŋ] | check |
| rijst (de) | [rɛjst] | rice |
| rode bes (de) | ['rɔdə bɛs] | redcurrant |
| rode biet (de) | ['rɔdə bit] | beetroot |
| rode peper (de) | ['rɔdə 'pepər] | red pepper |
| rode wijn (de) | ['rɔdə wɛjn] | red wine |
| rogge (de) | ['rɔxə] | rye |
| room (de) | [rõm] | cream |
| rosse populierenboleet (de) | ['rɔsə popʉ'lirən·bolēt] | orange-cap boletus |
| rozijn (de) | [rɔ'zɛjn] | raisin |
| rum (de) | [rʉm] | rum |
| rundvlees (het) | ['rʉnt·vlēs] | beef |
| russula (de) | [rʉ'sʉla] | russula |
| saffraan (de) | [saf'rān] | saffron |
| salade (de) | [sa'ladə] | salad |
| sap (het) | [sap] | juice |
| sardine (de) | [sar'dinə] | sardine |
| saucijs (de) | ['sɔsɛjs] | vienna sausage |
| saus (de) | ['saus] | sauce |
| schaaldieren | ['sxal·dīrən] | crustaceans |
| schapenvlees (het) | ['sxapən·vlēs] | lamb |
| schil (de) | [sxil] | peel |
| schoteltje (het) | ['sxoteltʃə] | saucer |
| selderij (de) | ['sɛldɛrɛj] | celery |
| serveerster (de) | [sɛr'vērstər] | waitress |
| sesamzaad (het) | ['sɛzam·zāt] | sesame |

| | | |
|---|---|---|
| sinaasappel (de) | ['sināsapəl] | orange |
| sinaasappelsap (het) | ['sināsapəl·sap] | orange juice |
| sla (de) | [sla] | lettuce |
| smaak (de) | [smāk] | taste, flavor |
| snede (de) | ['snedə] | slice |
| snoek (de) | [snuk] | pike |
| snoekbaars (de) | ['snukbārs] | pike perch |
| snoepje (het) | ['snupjə] | candy |
| soep (de) | [sup] | soup |
| soja (de) | ['sɔja] | soy |
| spaghetti (de) | [spa'xeti] | spaghetti |
| specerij , kruiderij (de) | [spesə'rɛj], [krœydə'rɛj] | spice |
| spek (het) | [spɛk] | bacon |
| spiegelei (het) | ['spixəl·ɛj] | fried eggs |
| spinazie (de) | [spi'nazi] | spinach |
| spruitkool (de) | ['sprœyt·kōl] | Brussels sprouts |
| steur (de) | ['stør] | sturgeon |
| stuk (het) | [stʉk] | piece |
| suiker (de) | [sœykər] | sugar |
| suikerbakkerij (de) | [sœykər bakə'rɛj] | confectionery |
| taart (de) | [tārt] | cake |
| tandenstoker (de) | ['tandən·'stɔkər] | toothpick |
| tarwe (de) | ['tarwə] | wheat |
| thee (de) | [tē] | tea |
| theelepeltje (het) | [tē·'lepəltʃə] | teaspoon |
| tomaat (de) | [tɔ'māt] | tomato |
| tomatensap (het) | [tɔ'matən·sap] | tomato juice |
| tong (de) | [tɔŋ] | tongue |
| tonijn (de) | [tɔ'nɛjn] | tuna |
| ui (de) | ['œy] | onion |
| varkensvlees (het) | ['varkəns·vlēs] | pork |
| veenbes (de) | ['vēnbɛs] | cranberry |
| vegetariër (de) | [vəxɛ'tarier] | vegetarian |
| vegetarisch | [vəxɛ'taris] | vegetarian |
| vermout (de) | ['vɛrmut] | vermouth |
| vers geperst sap (het) | [vɛrs xə'pɛrst sap] | freshly squeezed juice |
| verse kruiden | ['vɛrsə 'krœydən] | greens |
| vetten | ['vɛtən] | fats |
| vijg (de) | [vɛjx] | fig |
| vis (de) | [vis] | fish |
| vitamine (de) | [vita'minə] | vitamin |
| vlees (het) | [vlēs] | meat |
| vliegenzwam (de) | ['vlixən·zwam] | fly agaric |
| voorgerecht (het) | ['vōrxərɛht] | appetizer |
| vork (de) | [vɔrk] | fork |
| vossenbes (de) | ['vɔsənbɛs] | cowberry |
| vrucht (de) | [vrʉxt] | fruit |
| vruchten | ['vrʉxtən] | fruits |
| vulling (de) | ['vʉliŋ] | filling |
| wafel (de) | ['wafəl] | waffles |
| walnoot (de) | ['walnōt] | walnut |
| water (het) | ['watər] | water |

| | | |
|---|---|---|
| watermeloen (de) | ['watərmɛ'lun] | watermelon |
| whisky (de) | ['wiski] | whiskey |
| wijn (de) | [wɛjn] | wine |
| wijnglas (het) | ['wɛjn·xlas] | glass |
| wijnkaart (de) | ['wɛjn·kãrt] | wine list |
| wild (het) | [wilt] | game |
| witte wijn (de) | ['witə wɛjn] | white wine |
| wodka (de) | ['wɔdka] | vodka |
| worst (de) | [wɔrst] | sausage |
| wortel (de) | ['wɔrtəl] | carrot |
| yoghurt (de) | ['jogʉrt] | yogurt |
| zalm (de) | [zalm] | salmon |
| zeevruchten | [zē·'vrʉxtən] | seafood |
| zoet | [zut] | sweet |
| zoete kers (de) | ['zutə kɛrs] | sweet cherry |
| zonder gas | ['zɔndər xas] | still |
| zonnebloemolie (de) | ['zɔnəblum·'ɔli] | sunflower oil |
| zout (het) | ['zaut] | salt |
| zure kers (de) | ['zʉrə kɛrs] | sour cherry |
| zure room (de) | ['zʉrə rõm] | sour cream |
| zwarte bes (de) | ['zwartə bɛs] | blackcurrant |
| zwarte koffie (de) | ['zwartə 'kɔfi] | black coffee |
| zwarte peper (de) | ['zwartə 'pepər] | black pepper |
| zwarte thee (de) | ['zwartə tē] | black tea |

www.ingramcontent.com/pod-product-compliance
Lightning Source LLC
LaVergne TN
LVHW051730080426
835511LV00018B/2986